DEDICATION

The year was 1946 when two dozen cotton mill hands gathered at Byers Field to play baseball for their final season. Social and economic changes in the wake of World War II caused the team's demise as well as the break-up of East Alabama Industrial League made up of several other textile mill sponsored teams.

Mystic Bat is dedicated to that devoted group of men who alternated playing baseball with eight-hour shifts in the mill so that villagers could enjoy America's greatest pastime close to home. I am forever grateful to this team that provided me the opportunity to experience one of the happiest times of my life—the team's batboy. Without that final season this work of fiction would not have been possible. Many thanks to the following members of that Avondale Mills team from the Bevelle Village:

Frank Birchfield, Pete Blankenship, Wendell Boos, Gaines Coker, Max Davis, Joe Florine, --Hodnett, Troy Holley, "Dutch" Holman, Elmer Hassett, James Limbaugh, David McCollough, "Hook" Newman, Howard Rhodes, "Dodie" Thurman, Lewis Truett, Johnny Trussell, "Shorty" Vickers, and Harrell Vickers. Other personnel were Robert Graves, Athletic Director; Clyde Whetstone, Scorekeeper; and Umpires Abbie Hall and Herman Smith.

Source: Janet W. Seaman's collection of autographed baseballs.

Acknowledgements

The mere passage of time serves to soften one's memories and smooth the edges of actual events. For that reason, I owe a sincere debt of gratitude to Tim Cobb who read the manuscript and offered corrections and suggestions. Laura Dykes Oliver spent untiring hours poring over photos and memorabilia to sharpen my recollections.

I appreciate Cindy Church's comments following her reading the manuscript through the eyes of the daughter of former major leaguer, "Bubba" Church.

Thanks to Jason Mayfield, a middle-school teacher in Shelby County, Alabama who shared the manuscript with his gifted students whose abbreviated comments are appreciated:

"I love how your book takes me back in time and makes sense of that era."

"I really like Buck's dad J. R. because he talks to Buck like he is a real person, not a little kid.

"I am not a baseball fan, but this really good book has left me begging for more."

Thanks to Trey Sullivan, a student at Alabama School of Fine Arts, for his critique:

"The story is great! I enjoyed the history included in this story of the mill village and what it was like for an eighth-grader who loves baseball to live there."

Special thanks to Janet W. Seaman for her thoughtful comments and edits.

Finally, I appreciate Janelle Whetstone for her support in so many ways especially for photographing and designing the cover. Also, I greatly appreciate the contributions to crafting the cover by Ray Newton, Rob Whetstone, Leigh Hood and Mickey Newsome.

For Frances Moore, my friend

MYSTIC BAT

Bob Whetstone
May 16, 2013

By

Bob Whetstone

Other Novels by Bob Whetstone

Grave Dancin' **(2006, 2008, 2011)**

Crystal Angel: The Church and the Civil Rights Struggle in the South (2008)

Goober Joe: Coming of Age~~A Civil War Novel (2008)

Cotton Mary (2011)

For additional information go to www.bobwhetstone.com

The characters in this story are fictional and not intended to represent anyone living or dead.

ISBN: 978-1-105-62509-1

Published by Lulu Enterprises

www.lulu.com

PROLOGUE

I was forbidden to ever tell this story to anyone. My dad feared they'd think I belong in a loony bin, that I'd be locked up for keeps. But considering that you have obviously picked up my book and have begun reading, I'll let you in on what happened during possibly the best year of my life, 1947. Now I'm not talking 'bout a normal year, like from New Year's Day to December thirty-first. No sir, 'cause there's no baseball in the dead of winter, 'cept maybe in South America or Cuba. But in the mill village where I grew up, the year always began in early spring, ushered in by the first crack of a bat, the first smack of a fist in a glove and the first dusting of a rosin bag on a pitcher's fingers. My memory of that magical time is as clear as the creek water that runs behind the right field fence at Briers Field. This story is mine and it begins on a breezy March day, the day I hear that the old ballpark is being demolished.

Buck Clinton

CHAPTER 1

My buddy Tad comes running up to where I'm busting up lumps of coal in our backyard, all huffing and puffing like something's on fire in the village. "Buck, you gotta haul off and come with me to the ballpark. They're tearing it down."

"Oh, no!" I drop the ax and shake the coal dust off my hands before I grab his overalls bib. "You'd better not be lying to me, Tad, if you know what's good for you."

"I ain't lying, my mother saw somebody taking the big sign off the roof this morning when she came in from work." He pries away my grip and takes off running. "Let's go see 'fore it's all tore down." I follow him, jump the blue dye ditch next to the road and head for Briers Field. If the huge brick cotton mill didn't stand in our way, it would be a short run.

"See, I told you," Tad points to the rusting tin roof of the grandstand as we finally top the rise leading down to the field. "Look, the sign's gone and do you hear all that hammering going on?"

My heart sinks to think the mill owners have decided to do away with baseball. The war had borrowed most of our team, but now that the players are back, there's no reason the Cherokee Mill Chiefs can't take the field again. Tad slows down and stops in the dust. I look back and motion him forward.

"Come on, let's go watch."

7

Tad shakes his head slowly from side to side, his face crimps up like he's winding up to cry. "Are you crazy? I can't stand to watch it. You know we'll hafta spend the summer without seeing any baseball. What'll we do?"

"But we can still have lots of fun rounding up enough boys to play shove-up, can't we?" Not looking at his sad face, afraid of catching his mood, I try to cheer him up.

"Yeah, and where would we play, in old man Anthony's pasture with stinking cow pies for bases? You go on, I'm going back home." Tad turns away to hide his tears and then scuffs his feet through the dry sandy dirt along the path we came from.

Looking down the hill I stare in disbelief at a long dark stripe across the mottled roof. The big white Briers Field sign with faded green letters has left its shadow behind. The hammering stops and in that moment of silence I feel a strange force drawing me into the grandstand despite its padlocked doors and waist-high weeds guarding the ticket windows. A warning echoes in my head, *Go away, young man, don't look at me. You must'nt see me like this, all broken down inside, ready for the scrap pile!* I have an urge to turn and catch up with Tad, but something strange, like a magnet draws me close to the field. The voice I hear changes its tune, *All right Buck, come on in, save me if you can, it's my last chance."*

I feel two forces, one pushes me away from my favorite spot on earth and the other pulls me closer begging for help. Startled by a loud crack from inside the grandstand, I picture the whole back wall being torn down. I strain to hear more, but the only sound is the hum from the cotton mill behind me.

I catch a glimpse of a small corner of the ticket window, not quite hidden by tall weeds. It's open. Driven by some unknown force I plow through the winter-browned growth until I reach the tiny green door. As I pull back the long-rusted hinges give way and the door crashes at my feet. I prop the freed door securely against the wall, place my foot on the top edge and poke my head through the opening.

"Wanna buy a ticket?" The gruff voice from inside breaks the silence. A sharp pain streaks across the back of my head as my foot slips off the fragile perch and I tumble into the weeds.

"Watch out, son. Did you hurt yourself?" The mill's handyman peers through the ticket window.

"No, sir," I look up from the ground at Mr. Holley, rubbing my head in search of a bump.

"As long as you're here, son, come on 'round to the bleachers gate and help me move the sign."

"Sign?"

He doesn't answer and I don't hesitate. I scoot around the grandstand and down a trail to the players' gate behind the visiting team's dugout. Once inside the park, I scan the outfield from right to left and back again. The faded green fence, missing a few boards, flashes a snaggle-toothed grin. Just as a baseball game past the fifth inning, it appears tearng down Briers Field is official and in the record book. Somebody has harrowed up the infield leaving clumps of white in front of the grandstand around home plate. The pitcher's mound is pulverized, flattened like it's for softball.

Mr. Holley resumes his hammering, so I step into the grandstand, hankering to keep my visit short. Now I know how our soldiers feel in those Movietone films at the Strand Theatre when they step into a bombed out cathedral. Scattered rows of the faded green seats that form a half-bowl up the hillside are ripped out. The tin roof slants upward toward the field then angles down over the ground level box seats directly behind where home plate used to be. Chicken wire that once protected the fans from foul balls now hangs like a tattered and frayed veil masking a grief that lies within. Pigeons flutter from the rafters to protest my intrusion.

"Make haste, Buck, 'fore the shadows cover my work," Mr. Holley calls from the middle section of seats. "I need help turning this sign over so I can paint the other side."

No backing down now, I go to help. The sign leans against a complete row of seats. A fresh coat of paint covers the old lettering and the smiley-face baseball. Mr. Holley hands me two rags and warns of fresh paint. We struggle to reverse the heavy sign.

"What are you doing to the sign?"

"Just sprucing it up a bit." For what, I wonder. He dips a brush into the paint and goes to work on the unpainted side. "Stand back so you won't go home speckled like a Dominecker chicken."

Again, the urge to leave arises but curiosity scores and I remain to watch him drag a streak of white behind each carefully aimed stroke. I drop the rags and wander up the steps searching for some clue to the fate of Briers Field. Reaching the top I closely search the field and spot a tall silver needle pointing to the sky where once a brown telephone pole had stood just outside the center field fence. I hop down the steps to ask Mr. Holley what he knows about it.

"Did you do that by yourself?" I ask, pointing to the shiny new flagpole.

"It's not much to brag about. It don't take Patton's army to slap a fresh coat of paint on a fifteen foot sign," he says, wiping his hands with mineral spirits.

"No sir, I mean the flagpole."

"Oh, that. Well, I painted it and the city crew set it up."

Just like when my dad drove in a run to break a tie in the bottom of the ninth, a flood of hope bubbles up inside me. So, it seems the grandstand is getting fixed up instead of torn down. Not to let my imagination run wild, I recall the ballpark was the site of many events besides baseball—rodeos, boxing matches, circuses, and July Fourth barbeques. Maybe Briers Field is being spruced up for something besides baseball. After all, the mill still has no team, even though the war is over.

"O.K., son, I'm done here for now. You can help me tote my stuff to the truck, if you've a mind to. Just leave the paint can so I can add another coat when it dries."

He unties the denim carpenter's apron and folds it over his hand-made tool box covering a crowbar, a hammer, a brace-and-bit and some chisels. Aren't these the tools of destruction?

"Here," he hands me the paint brush and rags and points to his truck parked behind the home team dugout. He shoves the toolbox into the truck bed and slams the tailgate. "Git in, son, I'm headin' pretty close to your house. Just set that stuff on the floorboard."

Here's my chance to ask Mr. Holley about the plans for the field. I pull open the door that's emblazoned with the Cherokee Mill Indian head. Mr. Holley lays a piece of burlap across the seat to cover a loose spring. "The mill promised me a new truck now that the war's over. This baby's been working nigh onto seven years and it's time for her to retire."

He starts the motor and shifts into low gear. "I need to take a turn around the fence to count the number of planks I have to replace." He heads across the plowed-up infield toward the left field bleachers. "Termites got into most of 'em." When I notice a stack of new lumber near the left field bleachers, I start to ask a question but Mr. Holley shushes me and continues to count.

He stops the truck and writes the number down on a scrap of wood. I screw up enough courage to ask, "What's all that new lumber for over there?" I point across the field.

"New fence boards, new seats in the grandstand and a little patching up on the ticket window door you busted," he laughs.

"But I. . ."

"Yeah, yeah, just pulling your leg. Rust already took care of them hinges. Superintendent Plummer told me to get this place fixed up by April Fools' day. 'Drop everything and get it done,' he said, so it's at the top of my list."

"Then what's happening?"

"Don't rightly know. The Super ain't obliged to tell me why he wants something done. I just do it. No questions asked." He steers the truck through the open gate near right field. "No use closing the gate. Anybody can get in with them fence boards down."

No chance to ask more questions. Mr. Holley chatters on like a fired up infielder about the repairs he's made to each house we pass on the way to the maintenance gate behind the mill. "I'll let you out here, son." He stops the truck at the closed gate. "Wait a minute. I've got something here you might like." He reaches behind the seat and pulls out a baseball bat. "I found this stuck in the dugout wall where I tore out the rotten boards."

"O boy, a Louisville Slugger!" I rub my fingers along the ash handle worn smooth by some player's rough hands. I can almost hear the pop of hard horsehide against the wood as the ball carries far over the fence and the fans go wild. It's a home run. "And it's not even broke."

"I'm much obliged for your help and your company, son. If that bat could talk, it could tell you all you'd ever want to know about Cherokee Mill baseball and the Industrial League we played in. I doubt we'll ever see them good ol' days again."

I jump out of the truck to take a few practice swings with my own bat. When I turn around to thank the handyman, he has already pulled the truck into the mill yard. I study the bat in my hands more closely and begin to read the trademark on the barrel. Before I can finish reading the printed letters they change shape and run together forming a smiling face. I blink my eyes again and again. The face is still there. "Ol' timer, I wish you could talk." I Look around to be sure no one hears me and when I ask, "Can you tell me if the mill's gonna start up a baseball team again?" the face is gone. I see only the Louisville Slugger trademark. This is really weird. My mind's playing tricks on me 'cause I'm wishing too hard. Just to get my head straight again, I swing the bat overhead a few times like I'm on deck waiting for my turn at bat. As I rest the bat on my shoulder it begins to vibrate like it has a motor inside. Then I hear a muffled voice in my head say, *Baseball's coming back soon.* The bat is still again. I strut towards home like a Cherokee Mill Warrior coming up to the plate.

Chapter 2

No sooner'n I step onto Laurel Street, my sisters spy me from our front porch and run up flinging questions at me faster than balls flying in a pepper game.

"Where'd that bat come from, Buck? Can I see it? Is it heavy? Did Daddy buy it for you? I wanna play with it," they bug me, the way little sisters know how to do.

"It's not a toy. Anyway, girls and baseball don't mix." I grip the handle tighter to stress it's my new property. I try to lift the bat off my shoulder to take a practice swing, just to make my point, but it won't budge. It feels like someone is standing behind me holding it down. I spin around. Nobody's there.

"What'cha doing, Buck, dancing with that old bat?" giggles Bobbie Jean.

Flustered and bothered, I conjure up a weak excuse, "Naw, I'm, I'm 'bout to see how good it swings."

Still giggling, Bobbie Jean takes our younger sister's hand and skips toward the house. She hollers over her shoulder, "Daddy's at the clubhouse playing dominoes and Mother said if you ain't home when he gets back, it'll be the devil to pay." Though I bear the cross of having two little sisters, it's better than having older ones to boss me around.

I make plenty of room of between us so I can test this crazy bat again. I jiggle it around when, to my surprise, it slides off my shoulder with ease. Was it protecting the girls or did my muscles suddenly give way? What's going on with this bat?

I follow my sisters on across the footbridge that covers the fieldstone ditch between the road and our yard, the ditch flowing with denim blue waste water from the dye vats in the mill. Some say the warm blue liquid is poisonous, but most kids swear it's good for curing ringworm, itch and athletes foot and sometimes it's just plain fun to have blue feet and blue hands. However, my mother put a stop to my ditch wading one morning when she found my bed sheets had turned blue. My sisters still sneak outside and color their old socks in the run-off using Dad's fishing pole.

"Don't come dragging that old bat in this house. Leave it on the porch where it belongs," Mother yells from the kitchen. She claims Dad and I, she calls us her boys, try to crowd her and the girls out of our little brown shotgun house with our collections of baseball stuff. Every now and then she throws up her hands and declares, "Three little rooms and one tiny closet don't leave much room. I have to go outside just to change my mind." Renting a creosote stained house from the mill is far from my mother's dream of a decent home.

Sometimes when we catch Mother in a good mood she tells the story of how she met Daddy at Briers Field. "Your daddy chased a pop foul and dropped it right in front of my seat in the bleachers." Then Dad would say, "Yeah, I missed the ball, but I caught your mother instead. Fair trade, I'd say." After they got married and we kids came along, my dad worked the first shift so he could play on the mill team and Mother pulled third shift duty while we slept. Until that day Dad limped home from the Army, men mill hands and baseball players were one and the same to me.

"Where'd this come from?" Dad yells from the front door.

Mother answers, "It doesn't belong in here, so leave it be." Her demand comes too late. The screen door squeaks and bangs against the doorframe followed by a house-shaking slam of the front door.

"I tell you, J. D., one day you're gonna slam that door and this whole chicken coup'll fall in," she says. "Your boy brought that bat home, so ask him." Mother gives up her claim on me whenever she thinks Dad and I conspire to set her on edge. Dad hands me the bat and greets my sisters with big hugs.

"Y'all are almost too big to pick up anymore," he says as they squeal at being lifted tip-toe.

"Watch out for your leg, J. D., you can hardly stand on it much less tote two growing girls," Mother warns.

"Daddy, make Buck let us see his bat," Annie whines, "He won't even let us touch it."

Daddy gives me a look that says, "Don't make me get into this spat," so I offer the business end of the bat to Annie. "Here, it's just an old Louisville Slugger. Hop on it and ride around the house for all I care."

With me gripping the tapered handle, Annie lifts her hand, but stops short of touching it. She backs away slowly. "Don't care 'bout it now," she sniffs. I point the bat towards Bobbie Jean, but she clasps her hands behind her back and shakes her head. Both girls glare at the bat as though it has turned into a cottonmouth.

"Come on girls, he won't hit you with it," Dad says. He takes hold of the big end. "That's no way to hand somebody a baseball bat, son. Here, let me show you." Dad tries to pull it out of my hands, but my fingers curl even tighter around the handle. "Turn it loose, Buck. Let me have it."

"I'm trying, but I can't let go." My fingers freeze and begin to ache. Fear creeps into my bones, not from Dad's flaring temper, but from what this pigheaded bat is doing to me.

"You let go the bat, son or I'll take my belt to you," Dad says, his face reddens, nose flares. The girls sidle over to Mother, the three of them watching the tug-o-war in silence.

I shake my head from side to side trying to think of words to explain my rebellious hands. Dad blurts, "O. K., son. I'll teach you to disobey your daddy." Dad releases the big end of the bat and it begins to quiver out of control. He tries to grab hold again, but the elusive bat evades his grip.

"Be damned! Stop shaking it, Buck."

"I'm not doing it. I'm trying to let go."

"He's having a fit," Mother yells. "Buck, can you hear me?" Dad drops his hands and the bat stops shaking. He gives me a stern look and orders me to drop the bat.

"It's still stuck to my hands," I whisper, lowering the heavy end to the floor.

"Thank goodness," Mother says coming towards me. "Let me see if he has a fever."

"Look me in the eye, son. Where'd you get this bat, Where'd you find it?" I was too shaken to answer him. "Go put on some hot water, Mary. We'll wash off this sticky stuff."

Mother removes her hand from my brow. "He's got no fever, J. D." Then she hurries to the kitchen with my sisters tagging along. As soon as they leave the room, the bat releases its grip and drops to the floor with a thud. Dad rubs my palms. "Lord help us, I don't feel anything sticky."

"No sir, but my hands are real sore."

I kneel to get a closer look at the cantankerous bat. "Wait, don't touch it yet," Dad yells. He pulls a handkerchief from his back pocket and draws it across the handle. Then he rubs it up and down the length of the bat.

"Water's 'bout ready," Mother calls from the kitchen.

Gaining confidence, Dad lifts the bat by the handle and examines it closely. "There's a number on the end," I say, "looks like '36'".

"Yeah, it's one of those long boomers, thirty-six inches. Not many players use one this long. In fact, I knew one. . .wait a minute." Dad licks his thumb and rubs away the dark film covering the number. He drops his lower jaw and shakes his head slowly.

"Water's hot, but not scalding," Mother says as she enters the room holding a kettle with steam drifting from the spout. My sisters hang back in the doorway reluctant to come anywhere near the bat again.

"Don't need it now," Dad says, "But, keep it on the stove, just in case. Buck and I are gonna have a little talk 'bout where this bat come from, so y'all just go on in the kitchen and get supper ready, leave us alone for a while."

Dad walks over to the fireplace and pokes the dying coals, his customary move, buying time to think. "Always put your mind in gear before you start running your mouth," he's said to me ever since I can remember. Finally, he sits on the edge of my cot and turns the numbered end of the bat toward me with his foot. He motions for me to sit on the floor.

"Let's talk about this bat, son. Tell me everything from the first time you saw it 'til you brought it to the house."

I explained about going to Briers Field, leaving out the part about some force drawing me there. "Just skip everything 'til you come to the part about the bat."

"That won't take long, but I thought you'd wanna know what Mr. Holley was doing there."

"Maybe I do, but later."

"Mr. Holley found the bat and gave it to me. I brought it home and left it on the porch like Mother said."

"Did he say where he found it?"

"Oh, I forgot that part. Well, he ripped out some boards in the dugout and saw it stuck in there."

"The Chiefs' dugout?"

"Yessir."

Dad smiles, then chuckles, then he breaks out in a big belly laugh, so hard and long that tears run down his cheeks. "That son-uv-a-gun, that sneaky son-uv-a-gun," he says, shaking his head. After a few deep breaths, Dad's mood shifts and his tears turn bitter, no longer flowing from a well of joy.

"You know, son, I knew he did it, but I forgot about it 'til now." Dad finally settles down enough to talk. "Do you know whose bat this is, or was?" I shake my head. "See this initial scratched on the end. It's an 'M'. This bat was Frog McGee's, you know, Tad's daddy."

"No wonder Tad didn't go with me inside the grandstand, It probably made him sad about his daddy being dead."

"Frog was the only man on the team who used a bat this long. It was kind-a funny in a way, the shortest man on the team with the longest bat. But Frog was superstitious." Dad's mood begins to soften.

"What do you mean?"

"All us players had our little habits to scare off the demons that could spook our game. You know, like not stepping on the foul lines, keeping our caps on in the dugout, taking exactly three practice swings."

"Yes, sir, I remember, like Hook Slater always drew a circle around home plate with his bat."

"That's it. Well, Frog had a thing about this bat. He marked it with his initial because it. . .well, he. . .he claimed it talked to him," Dad's voice drops to a whisper.

"Talked to him?"

"Shhh, no need getting your mother upset," Dad continues in his lowered voice.

"Son, Frog McGee said this bat would tell him where to hit the ball before he went to the plate."

"That's weird, Dad. Did you believe him?" I try to keep my voice down.

"I played along and humored my ol' buddy even though I suspected that his head had caught too many bats on the back swing. He sure could get a hit though. He was the only hind-catcher in the league that hit in the clean-up spot. He was that good, bless his soul." Dad bows his head for a moment.

"Did Mr. McGee know you thought he, well, that he was a little off the beam?"

"Being good friends made it possible to put up with each other's quirks most of the time. That's why we got along so well." Dad pauses and absentmindedly picks up the bat. I cringe expecting something awful to happen.

"But that last game we played before we went to the Army was different. During batting practice he told me that he'd prove his bat was magic." Dad traces the circle around the trademark with his finger.

"Magic, you mean like a magician?"

"More like Madame Elaine, the fortune teller out on River Road. Anyway, he got real serious and pulled me over behind the dugout. He said, 'J. D., since this is our last game together, I'm gonna prove my bat tells me where to hit the ball.' That's exactly what he did. He moved out to the on-deck circle, bat in hand, and got down on his knee, real still, for about a minute. Most folks thought he was praying, but I knew better. He was listening to his bat talk to him. Just before he stepped up to the batter's box, he came over to the dugout and dusted his palms with rosin. That's when he whispered the bat's message in my ear."

"Did it work out?" I edge closer to Dad and the bat.

"Just like he said, almost exactly like he said. First time up he was supposed to fly out to left field. He did just that. Second time up he predicted a hit to short center field and he rifled a shot over second base. Sixth inning, with a man on first, he said he'd hit a grounder to short and get on base with a fielder's choice. He hit the ball so hard the shortstop couldn't handle it, so he was safe on first after all."

"Did that count? I mean, did the bat make an error too?"

"He just acted like it was supposed to happen that way." Dad gets real quiet as I wait on edge for the rest of the story. Finally he continues, "The last time Frog came up to bat we were two or three runs behind with the bases loaded."

"Supper's ready," Mother calls from the kitchen. "Y'all get washed up and come on."

"We'll be there directly," Dad replies.

"Son, do you remember that game with Sycamore, the last one we played before the team broke up?"

"I only remember Mr. McGee got into a fight with the umpire after the game."

"There was a scuffle, but it was in the ninth inning. I hate to go on about Frog McGee like this, him being, you know, not with us anymore. Let's go wash up for supper." Dad lays the bat on my cot, but on second thought, he stands it in the corner and stares for a few minutes.

"Tell me the rest of the story, about Mr. McGee's fight with the umpire."

"I don't know, son. I have to ponder what really happened some more. And you being friends with Tad makes me think twice about telling his dad's story. It may not be fair to him."

"I won't say a word to Tad, Dad, I promise, scout's honor."

"Buck, my boy, you'll have to do more than that if I reveal the mystery of this bat. You'll have to promise never to tell a single soul, you can't, for your own good."

"My own good?"

"Come on, let's eat. We'll talk a spell after supper."

Chapter 3

Talk around the supper table is strangely quiet tonight. Right after Dad says the blessing, Mother puts a damper on chatter. "I reckon y'all left that baseball bat in the house after all." Dad takes a quick bite of cornbread to allow time to let her accusation hang in the air just long enough to lose its buoyancy.

"Mighty good cornbread, Mother," he says before tasting the beans.

"Fixed it like always," she retorts, casting a suspicious eye first at him, then at me. Mother forgoes sharing her usual sanitized versions of talk around the spooler room. The girls take her cue and anxiously wait to hear the secrets Dad and I shared earlier. I scarf down my food, the first one with a clean plate, but I'm not allowed to leave the table until everyone is finished eating. Mother and Bobbie Jean dawdle over their food as I stare at the other empty plates on the table.

Dad finally breaks the tedious mood. "I heard some talk at the clubhouse today about a start-up baseball team." My heart skips a beat.

"I've heard enough about baseball today," Mother says, rising from her chair to clear leftovers from the table. "I'd just as soon you boys take that talk out of the kitchen and let me and the girls straighten up in here."

Dad chuckles, "Not much else to say, 'cept that's all I heard." With that, he wanders out to the back porch lifting a pack of Lucky Strikes from his shirt pocket. I jump up to follow him, full of anticipation.

He lights up with a flame of his Zippo and exhales curls of blue smoke into the cool night air. "Can't see all the Big Dipper this time of year, but there's the Little Dipper standing there with the North Star at the tip of its handle."

"Yessir, I see." With the cigarette between his fingers, Dad traces other constellations, Draco, Cassiopeia, Bootes, he continues, but my mind is not on astronomy tonight. I want to hear the rest of Mr. McGee's tale about the talking bat. "You heard somebody say the mill is gonna start a baseball team again?" I ask trying to steer the talk back to that last Chiefs game.

Dad snuffs out the cigarette stub on the bottom of his shoe, spreads the unburned tobacco on the ground and flips the paper into the garbage can. "Hold on, son, that's not exactly the way I heard it. There's a rumor that a team might be organized pretty soon, but not by the mill."

"You mean the players won't work in the mill? How can that be?"

"Settle down; let's back up before you make up a whomp-sided story. First, I'll say again exactly what I heard, and then I'll give my opinion so you won't confuse facts with cock-and-bull."

"Yessir." Dad tries my patience, but I have no choice except to listen closely.

"What I heard came from somebody I won't name. One of the boys I play dominoes with has a brother that works in a car dealer's body shop, which I won't name. He said a group of 'big mules' in town are trying to start a baseball league with a team from River Bend."

"Big mules?"

"Folks with money. And they're talking to towns that had cotton mill teams in the old industrial league that folded after the war started."

"Like Sylacauga?"

"And Lanett, Tallassee, Opelika, and even some across the State line in Georgia. But remember, that's just talk right now. It may depend on whether the mills will allow the teams to use their old ballparks for practice and home games. Some city parks are only large enough for American Legion ball."

"Is that why Mr. Holley is fixing up Briers Field?"

"Now that's the point where the information stops and speculation begins. Anyway, I'll tell you what I think, but you'll have to keep it to yourself and not go around spreading loose talk."

"Can't I even tell Tad?"

"I thought you'd get us back to Frog McGee's funny bat." I follow Dad into the back yard as he rubs his chin. Putting his arm around my shoulder, he continues. "I don't think it's a good idea to tell Tad anything about a ball team yet and get his hopes up. It's my hunch that those cotton mill owners will not fix up their old ballparks and some may be too run down to repair. I hear that Lafayette and Sycamore already tore theirs down. Without fields there's no league. With no league there's no use in having teams."

"But we could have mill teams again, just like before."

"No, I'm afraid everything's changed. The old cotton mill spirit went to war and never came back. Cherokee plans to sell their village houses and turn the school over to the City. They've already shut down the swimming pool. I reckon the clubhouse will be next."

"That don't seem right. Why can't I tell Tad?"

"You'll understand when I tell you what happened after that last game at Briers Field. It's what Frog McGee did with his bat."

"You mean talking to it?" I say remembing some words of my own I uttered to the bat earlier today.

"No, I mean hiding it in the dugout. We were supposed to turn in all the team's equipment after the game with Sycamore—balls, gloves, bats, uniforms, everything except our socks, spikes and caps. When we got to basic training, Frog told me that he hid his special bat behind the wall in the dugout so he would have it when he returned home after the war."

"You mean he stole the bat?"

"No, he just laid it by to make sure nobody fooled with it while he was gone. He thought somebody might break it or get hurt trying to swing it. When he never made it back to play ball again I completely forgot about the bat, until today."

"It sounds like Mr. McGee thought his bat was human, like a person, alive with feelings and a mind of its own. What do you think?"

Dad scratches his head and gazes at the starry sky again. "Don't rightly know, yet. So let's keep that bat's funny ways between us boys for a while, until I can figure out whether it's us or the bat that's crazy. No need to bring up Tad's sadness over his Dad's death all over again."

I think Dad is downright mystified. Maybe he figures the stars have the answer to the bat's mystery if he looks long enough. I count on him to explain anything I don't understand, but this bat has him stumped. He wants to believe Mr. McGee pulled his leg about listening to the bat, but now he's not sure. I intend to find out more. "What about the fight?"

"I was just thinking about that, son, trying to sort out what I saw and what Frog told me at boot camp. What I remember is we were at bat in the bottom of the ninth inning, three runs behind with two outs and the bases loaded. Frog McGee comes to the plate."

"Did he kneel down and listen to his bat before that?"

"I guess so, but I was on third base trying not to get picked off and didn't pay much attention to him."

"Did Mr. McGee get a hit?"

"Well, he did," Dad pauses, "and he didn't. At the crack of his bat, I started running not paying attention to where the ball went. As I crossed home plate, the umpire called it a foul ball, so I headed back to third. That's when everything got confused. Frog hollered, 'It's a home run, y'all keep on running.' So we all rounded the bases again."

"Did he really hit a home run?"

"Well, as I cross home plate again and turn to shake hands with Frog who is now rounding third, the crowd begins screaming and coming on to the field thinking the game is over. But it's not. When Frog crosses the plate, Smitty, the umpire gets right in his face and says, "Strike one, McGee. Now pick up your bat and get back to the plate. In all the commotion, I can only hear Frog argue that the ball nicked the foul pole and was fair, but the umpire orders him back to the batter's box. That's when all tarnation breaks out and we lose the game."

"But with only one strike, Mr. McGee had another chance, didn't he?"

"He did," Dad walks back to the steps and lights up another cigarette. "But he didn't. Frog does something he'd never done before. He pushes Smitty away so hard that he falls over home plate knocking the breath out of him. He doesn't get up right away. Frog picks up his bat and heads to the dugout. Some of the players help Smitty to his feet while I catch Frog by the arm and tell him it's a foul ball. He jerks away, picks his bat up and hollers, 'Fair ball! My bat don't lie! You and Smitty can go to hell.'"

"Is that when he hid the bat in the dugout?"

"Not then. People run out to pat him on the back, but when they see him holding that crazy bat with both hands and talking to it like a person, they back away to give him plenty of room. He tells Tad to pick up his mask, shin guards and chest protector and follow him out the gate like he'd won the game."

"I remember helping Tad with the equipment but not the part about the umpire being pushed down. Was he O. K.?"

"Yeah, when Smitty comes to, he looks around for Frog, calling him names I don't allow in my house. Frog is long gone, so Smitty declares the game a forfeit. That's how we lost."

"Is that all?"

"Frog and I were drafted and didn't have much to say after that until we settled in at Camp Blanding two weeks later. One day he follows me out of the mess hall and starts talking like he's worried about something. 'J. D., I want you to know I hid my baseball bat in the dugout behind the bench.' Then he says, 'I don't figure I'll make it back home when the war's over.' Well son, it's kind-a hard to explain the rest."

"You don't remember?"

"I remember all right, it's just that I forgot a promise 'til today."

"A promise?"

"Frog made me promise to tell his bat why he didn't come home," Dad whispers as though a big secret is about to surface.

"Are you gonna do it now, can I watch?"

"That's not all, son. He also wanted me to give his bat permission to hook up with another player when the team gets back together."

"Like you, Dad?"

"I think that's what Frog meant. He hoped his talking bat would transfer its power to me, but. . ." Dad rubs the shrapnel scar on his leg and shakes his head. "But my at-bat days are over and I won't be swatting anymore baseballs with any bat, especially that crazy one in the house."

"Maybe it will take up with me and I can play with the Dodgers one day."

"I'd be mighty proud if you do, son, but it appears you and that bat don't hit it off too good."

Mother sends Bobbie Jean to fetch us from the cool night air. Dad lingers behind to put out his smoke as I walk up the steps. "Buck," he says after my sister goes back inside. I turn around and watch as he zips his fingers across his lips and shakes his head.

"Yes sir."

Chapter 4

Sunday after church Mother orders me to get Mr. McGee's old bat out of the house. I wrap it in an empty flour sack and stash it under the house near the coal pile, safe from my sisters and out of Tad's sight in case he comes over to play. I curtain off a den with croaker sacks where I keep fishing worms, crickets, June bugs, snake skins and baseball cards, my own private hideout. After placing the bat on a rock pillar, I loop a strip of baling wire around it to hold it in place. I'm done with that contrary stick of hard ash for a while, at least until I can figure out the riddle of the baseball team.

Monday after school lets out, I make a bee-line for the ballpark to check on Mr. Holley's progress fixing up the place. Also, I can pick at him for information about the rumor Dad heard. I go through the right field gate and watch a man in overalls and a straw hat driving a team of mules around the infield. They drag a blanket made of logging chains to smooth out the crumpled dirt. Mr. Holley stands in center field fiddling with the top of a large feed sack. I trot out across the fresh cut weeds. "Looks like you got most of the fence boards done," I say, just to work up to asking about the phantom baseball team that haunts my dreams. "Looks dandy."

"Still needs paint," he says. "While you're here make yourself useful and grab a bucket." I pick up a galvanized bucket as he jerks one string that zips open the top of the sack.

I take a chance on popping a question. "I hear you're fixing up Briers Field for a new baseball team."

Mr. Holley pours grass seed into my bucket and then fills the other one. "You ought to believe nothing you hear and half of what you see, son, and let it go at that."

"Yessir." I know this handyman knows more than he's letting on, so I play along a bit.

"Now, let's strew this rye grass even-like all over this weed-studded outfield." He tosses a handful over a bare spot near the fence. "Don't worry 'bout spreading it too thick, I've got three more sacks in the dugout."

"It looks to me like you're getting this field ready for baseball, Mr. Holley, it sure does." I walk beside him strewing grass seed as we go.

"What'd I tell you 'bout believing only half of what you see?"

We walk a bit farther 'til I empty my bucket. I turn it over and sit on it. "In that case, I'll believe there's only one mule over there dragging those chains and I'll believe only one of us is gonna seed this outfield. So, I reckon I'll just sit here and watch you strew seeds and pretend I don't see that other mule."

Mr. Holley scratches his head, wipes a bead of sweat from his brow and sets his bucket down. He looks at me real hard and breaks out laughing. "Well, I swan, boy; you twisted my saying out of shape real good. Come on, let's finish up before dark catches us. I'll tell you what I know 'bout the new baseball team."

~~~~

I seem to be the only boy in the village interested in the newspaper's contest to name the new baseball team. It's a good sign that I could be the one to think up a good name for the team and win season passes for Dad and me. The last day to turn in a
~~~~

contest entry is today, Thursday, March 15th, 1947. I wrote it down and carried it in my pocket since I heard about the contest.

"Hey Tad, did you hear about the contest to name the team?" I asked as we line up for school.

"What team?"

"The new baseball team that's coming to town real soon. I thought you knew we're gonna get to see baseball games again at Briers Field."

"Oh, that team," he shrugs his shoulders.

"Yeah, and we can sit on top of the dugout again like we used to, and maybe catch a foul ball or two."

Tad screws up his chubby face like he just bit into a green persimmon and shakes his head. I press on hoping to get a rise out of my buddy. "What if somebody from the newspaper comes up to your house today and says, 'Tad, I'm counting on you to come up with a good name for the River Bend team,' what would you say?"

"That sure got your goat," Peggy Sue turns around and can't help throwing in her two cents worth.

"Bug out girl, we're talking boy business."

"I'll hush after you tell us what you'd call the team."

Peggy Sue stands her ground, which is to be expected. Her daddy played first base for the Chiefs and like Tad's daddy, he didn't make it home from the war. Being left handed like her daddy, she keeps his glove and takes every chance to play catch with us boys at the park. At first, we poked fun at her until we came up short of players one day and we let her hold down first base. If it wasn't for the dress, she played like a real first baseman.

"It's none of your beeswax what I'd call the team." Their argument is cut short by the bell that beckons us to the eighth grade classroom.

I cannot get my mind on schoolwork today. I scribble names of baseball teams followed by question marks and pass them back to Tad. At first he ignores the notes, but boredom sets in and he plays the game. Back and forth we go until health period comes before lunch. The mill's nurse shows up and takes the dozen girls to the auditorium to see a movie about personal things that boys make up secret stories about. Mr. Killibrew, our buttoned-up principal, teaches us boys a sanitized version of the girls' lesson by reviewing the Boy Scout Law and dwelling on the clean and reverent part. He ends the lesson with a sigh of relief that is echoed by thirteen boys in the room. He neglects to mention why girls make our brains curdle and our innards boil, but that suits us just fine. We were as afraid to hear it as he was to tell it. The way he asked if we had questions was a sure sign for us to keep quiet.

I jumped at the chance to change the subject to baseball. "Mr. Killibrew, do you know about the new baseball team coming to town?"

The principal presses his two chins against his chest and peers over the spectacles perched on the end of his nose. He glances at me and then turns his head to stare out the open window as if he had not heard the question. In a moment, he answers like he's speaking to the tree outside the window. "Yes, I understand from the newspaper that our town is on the verge of hiring some professional baseball players to make up a team. It all depends on how many folks buy season tickets," he says with no more enthusiasm than he'd recited the scout law.

"You gonna buy one, Mr. Killibrew?" Tad asks.

"Didn't give it much thought, Tad. I don't allow much time for recreational pursuits beyond reading good books."

"Me neither," Tad says slumping down in his seat.

"You can get two free passes just for coming up with a name for the team," I offer. "I'm sure you'll win 'cause it'll take a real smart man like you to come up with a good team name."

Looking amused, Mr. Killibrew pulls his coat back, sticks his thumbs in his vest and turns away from the window to survey the half-empty room. "I think I'll leave naming the team to those whose summers drift by on zephyrs of hopelessness, like you young lads."

Not sure if we'd been insulted or praised, I ask, "Can we spend the rest of the period working on a name for the team?"

"Perhaps that would be a good exercise for your minds. One of you may win the tickets."

I spread my last sheet of paper across the desk. Tad leans over and with his huge hand prints a name in large letters: MILLERS. He signs his name, wedges the pencil behind his ear and returns to his seat. I stifle the urge to laugh as I stare at the ridiculous name. "Hey Tad, what's a 'Miller' anyway."

"Men that work in the mill, stupid, like our daddies, I mean, like mine used to."

"I thought they're called 'lint-heads'."

"That ain't nice," he whispers. "There're two cotton mills in River Bend and that's what most people do 'round here, work in a mill."

"Yeah, but, but I never heard of any kind of team called 'Millers', not baseball, football or basketball. Where'd you get that crazy idea?"

"It makes no difference to me if you like it or not. It fits."

The River Bend Millers. I repeat the name over and over in my mind. "I reckon I could get used to it, Tad," I say to be polite. "It rolls off my tongue. River Bend Millers win the pennant. Yeah, that just might work. Let's take it to the *Lookout* office after school. You might win the two season passes."

"Ain't got no use for free tickets. I don't like baseball anymore."

"In that case, I'll turn it in for you and maybe use your passes myself."

"Do what you want, Buck. I don't care." Tad says his last word on the subject.

I have to find some way to change Tad's mind about baseball before the season starts or Peggy Sue might take a notion to come sit on the dugout roof with me. It's nothing against Peggy Sue, 'cept she's the kind of girl I hate to like. A little taller than me, her skinny frame's rounding out quite nice and she catches and throws better 'n half the boys my age. Last summer her arms and legs stuck out like outfield fungos, but now, I don't know, guess I'd better keep my mind on Tad's weird team name.

After school, I run all the way to town only to be held up by the freight train lumbering through splitting the square down the middle. I glance at the bank's clock and wonder what time the newspaper office closes. I unfold the paper in my hand and read aloud, "River Bend Millers," with Tad's signature underneath. Such a silly name. With any luck the train will stop and I'll have an excuse to throw the paper away and head for home. The newspaper folks might laugh me right out of the building.

The caboose passes like a giant red gate turning people loose going in opposite directions down Main Street. Darting behind Carson's Drug Store, I take a shortcut down the alley to the newspaper office. I grasp the knob beneath the opaque glass door with arched lettering, *The River Bend Lookout,* but I do not turn it. Do I really want to do this? Tad's suggestion now seems more like it describes men like my granddaddy who grinds corn at his gristmill. Is Tad getting me back for liking baseball more than he does? Is he jealous? Where did he come up with *Millers* anyhow, from a Bugs Bunny cartoon?

I try to twist the doorknob but it won't budge. I hear voices inside the office. I stand still and listen, somewhat relieved that Mr. Craig has already locked up for the day. The question of River Bend Millers is dead in the water. The contest has ended for Tad, and me. A locked door is all that stands between me and free passes or total embarrassment.

I check the door once more and turn to walk home. Suddenly, the door squeaks and whines; a familiar voice rings out. "I thought I saw a shadow through the glass." Editor Craig, a friend of my Dad, stands there in his black suspenders and white shirt with loose tie, the same outfit he wore in the press box at Briers Field. "What can I do for you, son?"

Like a hobo caught stealing watermelons, I lose the words to explain why I'm standing here. "Door was locked," is all I can stammer out.

"We close up early on Thursdays after we put the paper out. What do you have for me, an item for next week's paper?" He points to the note paper in my hand.

There's no way out, so now I have to go through with it. "No sir, it's just an idea for the new baseball team. Is it too late?"

He tugs at the silver chain looped from his belt and lifts a pocket watch from a slit in his pants. "Not at all, not at all, it's not four o'clock yet. As a matter of fact, the contest judges are in my office right now. Bring it on in and give it to them yourself.

I walk inside and hear the lock click behind me. "Follow me," he leads me around the business counter through saloon-type swinging doors. "Pardon the clutter, son. We don't have much time for clean-up." The ink-splattered press is silent and small strips of lead letters lay scattered over a broad table as we approach Mr. Craig's office.

"Y'all want me to turn off the fan?" he asks three men struggling to hold a stack of letters and papers in place on a round table.

"Not unless you can convince Fuzzy to put out his cigar," replies the only man in a suit and tie.

"This young man brings in another entry for the contest. He wants to submit it in person." I cringe at Mr. Craig's twist on the truth, but step over to the man with the cigar. "Mr. Wetzel is President of the River Bend Baseball Club," he says gesturing to a red-cheeked man with thick rimless glasses. "These other gentlemen are Coley Farmer and Paul Alexander."

"Let's see what 'cha got there, boy." Fuzzy crushes the cigar stub into a glass ashtray with Hitler's face painted on a skunk's body. "If it's one of the major league mascots, we've already got 'em all except for the hapless Browns." His loose attitude convinces me the men will laugh at Tad's suggestion.

I offer Fuzzy the paper, but he only examines my face. "You look real familiar, boy. Did your folks buy a Studebaker from me?"

"No, sir, we don't have a car. My daddy works. . ."

"This is J. D. Clinton's boy," interrupts Mr. Craig, "used to play third base for the Chiefs."

"Oh yeah, I remember J. D.," says Fuzzy. "He was something else. Not many grounders got by him. If he got a glove on it, the batter was out," he says thrusting his thumb in the air imitating an umpire. "O-U-T, I mean. And he could hit a ball anywhere inside the park."

Fuzzy's remarks breaks open a floodgate of reminiscing among the four judges. "Do y'all remember Davey Long slamming into the centerfield fence and knocking himself cold?"

"Yeah, and now the poor fellow gets about in a wheel chair."

On and on they go with me standing there holding Tad's contest entry in my hand. Finally, a name comes up that grabs my attention.

"And what about that game-ending fight between Frog McGee and Smitty, Fuzzy says. He turns to me and asks, "Son, did your dad ever tell you what caused Frog to attack the umpire?"

The picture of Dad zipping his lips came to mind, so I stare at the floor. Mr. Craig intervened, "I understand McGee didn't tell anybody why he did it, took it to his grave. I interviewed him the day he left for the Army, but his response did not make sense."

"What'd he say?" asked Fuzzy.

"Nothing fit to print. He said if I want to know the truth, I could go talk to his bat, if I could find it." He turns to me. "So, little J. D., I suppose we're not taking care of your business by dwelling on long-gone days, are we?"

"That's all right, sir. This here's Frog McGee's boy's team name for the contest." I hand it to Fuzzy Wetzel. "I have to go home now."

Fuzzy unfolds the paper. "Let's have a look at Frog's boy's entry. H'mm, Millers." He repeats the name and grins.

"That's really different," says Coley Farmer.

I step just outside the office door to overhear their reactions.

"Don't believe I ever heard of a team with that name before," Paul Alexander says.

"Here, let me check the teams in this record book," says Mr. Craig. "There's a team in Minneapolis called the Millerettes. No, wait, that was two years ago when they were leading their league with a record of. . ."

"But why Millerettes instead of Millers?" Coley Farmer asks.

"Because it's a lady's team, it says here."

"That settles it. We don't want our folks associating our team with a women's league, do we?" Fuzzy concludes.

"Surely there must be a men's team called Millers if there is a women's team. What else does the book say?"

"Hold on, Coley. I need to pull out another book."

I don't want to hear any more about Millers or Millerettes, so I wander to the front door. I am tired of listening to town leaders who didn't bother to ask me my name. To them I'm "son", "boy", "J. D.'s boy", and "Little J. D.", all common names but not me. I wait for Mr. Craig to unlock the front door and release me from that smoky den of big mules.

"Thank you for taking the trouble to submit an interesting suggestion for a team name." A roar of laughter from inside the office overpowers Mr. Craig's thanks. I leave just in time to miss any more teasing. "I hope to see you at the ball games, Buck. And bring your Dad, too." At least Carl Craig remembers my name.

~~~~

Dad shakes a copy of the *Lookout* in my face. "Try and guess the name of our new baseball team, Buck, take a guess." I make a futile grab for the paper. "No, no, you have to guess. Here, I'll give you a clue:"

The judges have selected a name for the River Bend Class D baseball team that is both unique and appropriate for our town. The name is steeped in history dating back to 1884.

"It must be 'Dodgers', Dad."

"Not even close, son. Here's another clue from the story in the paper." Dad reads some more:

A local schoolboy offered a suggestion to the judges that seemed at first to be far removed from our community. But upon closer examination, the judges realized the reasoning behind his choice.

No matter how much I protest, Dad keeps on limping around the room teasing me by reading short excerpts from the front page. My sisters giggle like they're in on the secret.

"Here's another clue for you, Buck:"
~~~~

The new River Bend team will have the same name as the team that gave Ted Williams his start in professional baseball.

A knock at the front door interrupts Dad's guessing game. Mother yells, "Come on in," but Mrs. McGee is already inside. Tad moseys in behind her. She slaps a folded copy of a newspaper with the back of her hand several times.

"I declare, I declare. Do y'all see what my boy's done, my little Tad-pole?" Dad waves both hands to shush her so he can continue his fun with me, but she cannot stop. "It's right here on the front page, his name and everything. He's picked the name for the baseball team and won two free tickets to every game."

"Millers?" I ask.

Dad looks puzzled and checks his paper. "It's the Millers all right. How did you know that, Buck?"

I glance at Tad standing behind his mother. His chubby lips draw tight trying to fight back a smile as she continues raving about his good luck. "And we're gonna show up at every game pulling for our Chiefs, I mean Millers." I wonder if Tad's mother changed his mind about baseball.

Dad pats Tad on the back, "You must feel pretty good, Tad, being the town's hero."

Tad looks down, shuffles his feet. "I dunno, ask Buck."

"What about Buck?"

"It's my doing, Dad. Tad came up with the name and I took it to the paper. Tad didn't want me to turn it in, so I guess he's sore at me now." Tad continues looking at his shoes. "When I left the newspaper office, the judges were laughing like they weren't too impressed with the name, so I figured they'd thrown it in the trash can. Mr. Craig even found a women's team in his book called 'Millerettes'."

"That's not what Mr. Craig wrote, listen:"

The name Millers dates back to 1884 when the Minneapolis Millers first organized a baseball team. That team won the Western League pennant in 1896 and remains a force to be reckoned with in professional baseball today.

"But, Mr. Alexander didn't warm up to the name and he runs one of the cotton mills," I continue to argue my case.

"That's odd," says Dad. "He's quoted right here saying, 'It is a most appropriate name for the River Bend baseball team since a majority of the working folks in our town are employed at one of the textile mills.' So, I guess he's pretty happy with Tad's call."

Tad stands aside watching our parents rejoice over his good news. I watch carefully not wanting to set off a fuse that might be seething in Tad's craw. I'm a little jealous that he'll have free tickets and I'll have to pay admission to the games.

Chapter 5

Poco Walker stretches his hairy arms up and grasps the crossbeam under the edge of the new dugout roof, a feat no shorter man can do. Leaning his rounded belly forward, he shoots a brown stream from his bulging jaw that spatters the dry red dirt. "Get a move on," he shouts to a small group of players passing by, "not gonna have no lard-butt pitchers on my team." He stirs the tobacco stained spot in the dirt with his cleats and grumbles. "Helluva time to start shaping up a team; should-a started weeks ago."

The new manager of the River Bend Millers sheds his cap to wipe the sweat from his brow. A silver ring of clipped hair encases a shiny dome on top of his head, evidence that his playing days are behind him. He replaces the cap and pulls his sagging pants over the belly that favored more food than exercise. From head to toe, Poco Walker exhibits an athlete's frame except for the middle.

A stray ball rolls between the dugout and grandstand where Dad and I watch the first practice of the season. "Whaddya want, an apron?" the manager yells at the first baseman who had let the ball skid between his legs. Mr. Walker picks up the ball and throws to the first baseman hard enough to make a loud pop in his glove.

Still looking toward first base, the aging manager says, "You got b'iness here or you just come to watch?" Not sure who he's talking to, Dad says nothing. Then he turns to face us and says, "Well, cat got ya tongue?"

Dad rises to speak, “Sir, my name is J. D. Clinton.” He steps onto the field and shakes the manager’s hand. They move out of earshot like I don’t know what they’re talking about.

Yesterday a man came by our house, stopped his ’41 Plymouth coupe out front and beeped his horn several time. Dad had just settled into the front porch swing to rest his bones, especially his grenade damaged leg. He tells me to see what the man wants, so I hurry to the driver’s side of the car. “Is this forty-two Laurel Street?” the man dressed in a white shirt, bow tie and straw hat asks.

“Yessir.”

“Is that J. D. Clinton sitting up there on the porch?”

“Yessir.”

“Run up there and tell him I need to have a word with him.”

“Well, sir, you see his leg starts to bother him this time. . .”

“Don’t you hear good, boy. Go fetch him now.”

Dad is already making his way down the steps, so I back away as he approaches the man who can’t shake the frown off his face. “Well, Dewey, what brings you down to the village?”

“Clinton, I’m here on business from the superintendent’s office.”

Making sure him and Dad don’t tread on common ground, the tight-lipped dandy wastes no time relaying the superintendent’s message. “Mister Poco Walker was in our office today making arrangements to use Briers Field for practice and home games. He needs a scorekeeper and Mr. Plummer said you might do.”

Dad straightens up and draws a deep breath. I hold mine. He runs his hand over his slick black hair, hitches up his lint-flecked overalls by the gallouses and says, "Tell you what, I'll be mighty glad to think it over and. . ."

"I just deliver the message, Clinton, not make promises." Dewey spits his words out like a well-oiled loom in the weave shed. "If you want to apply for the job, show up at the ballpark tomorrow after work and speak to Mr. Walker." With that farewell, the messenger cranks the motor, grinds the gear into first and adds a final note. "Mr. Plummer says the job doesn't pay, so don't quit work and don't miss a shift doing it."

He drives off without hearing Dad say, "Much obliged." Dad sits on the roadside rock wall and reads my mind. "I'll meet you after school tomorrow, Buck. We'll go to Briers Field together and see what a real professional team manager is like."

"Betcha britches, I'll be ready."

~~~~

While Dad and Poco talk business, blood ripples inside me like a creek after a rain. It's hard to realize I'm actually watching real bush leaguers chase fly balls and grounders, run laps and chatter to each other. A short, stout man built like I remember Frog McGee hits infield practice. His constant stream of orders has a sharp edge different from the syrupy smooth talk of River Bend folks. "All right, two in the dirt. Get two. Shape up you there at second. First base! For Pete's sake, how can you play second if you can't find first base?" The flush-face coach trots to first base and raises the infield fungo high in the air. "See! This here's first base. When a batter hits a grounder, he runs over here to this base," sounding like a teacher giving baseball lessons to kids. He tosses up a ball and hits it right at the second
~~~~

baseman. "Throw it to first so I can tell if you learned anything." The other infielders cover their laughing faces with their gloves as the ball zips between the second baseman's legs. "For crying out loud," the coach moans.

Two pitchers running laps slow down and stop to talk to a gaggle of girls ogling the team from behind the new grandstand chicken wire. Mr. Walker's booming voice cuts short their visit. "Two more laps, boys. When I'm ready to run a courtin' service you'll be the first to know. Now hit the ground running."

"But we did ten already," protests a runner passing in front of the dugout.

"I'm talking to the lovebirds, they're gonna need their strength. The rest of you guys get a drink and start throwing."

The manager leaves Dad and walks over to confer with the coach hitting infield practice. Dad waves me over to join him. Poco Walker heads our way, head down with his hands stuffed in the back pockets of the old Chiefs uniform. Dad says, "This is my boy, Buck, Mr. Walker."

He glances at me without breaking stride and takes a seat in the dugout. "Don't ever be a pitcher, kid," he says removing his cap. "All they think about is girls, goofing off and making headlines."

"Yessir."

"Now, how 'bout fetching that bucket over here." I wait for the last pitcher to take a drink and tote the half-full bucket to the manager. He stirs the smooth island of ice around with the metal dipper but before drinking he gouges a ball of wet tobacco from his cheek with his finger and drops it on the ground. Then he rinses his mouth with the first swig and spits it out before emptying the dipper. "Son, looks like I'm gonna need help taming that wild herd of mustangs out on the field. Your dad says you might know somebody who'd like to be the team's batboy."

I am both surprised and confused. Did Dad set me up to ask Tad, or some older kid to do the job? I wonder until Poco lifts his six-foot plus frame off the bench and cuts a crooked smile across his sweaty face. "Your dad tells me that you and him would make a good team, scorekeeper and batboy. What d'ya think, son? Shake on the deal?" He offers his right hand.

"Betcha britches!" I don't know how I manage to get my breathless dry mouth to say the words. Dad crooks his neck to remind me to say, "Thank you, Mr. Walker, thank you."

Gripping my limp hand, he says, "Poco, son, call me Poco. "Just hang around and watch for a while, then start work tomorrow."

Dad winks his approval and heads back towards the grandstand. I spy Peggy Sue Slater on the third row popping a cotton mollie into her dad's old first baseman's pad. Her hair is pulled back and tucked under a Chiefs baseball cap looking like she's hankering to come out and practice with the team. I grab a bat and swagger out to get a closer look at the man hitting infield so she'll realize I'm now part of the team.

Next day, I run all the way from school to Briers Field decked out in Dad's old baseball cap. The grandstand looks fresh dressed up in its new coat of dark green paint and new sign on the roof. A slick oilcloth banner waves from the overhang proclaiming, *HOME OF THE MILLERS.* Entering the players' gate, I spot Poco near the pitcher's mound. He screws up his face as I approach.

"Where've you been, batboy? You're an hour late." He scowls.

"In school," I reply as my balloon bursts.

"School?" He removes his cap and scratches his head in one smooth move. "Damn, I forgot you're still in school." My job's on the line. "When's school out?"

"At three, but I can hurry. . ."

"No, I mean for the summer. I need you full time."

"Three more weeks, I think."

Poco grimaces, "Com'on over." I follow him to home plate. "This here's our new batboy," he tells the round-faced man who hit infield practice. He's not much taller than me. "Tell him your name, son."

"Buck."

"This here's Flip. He'll show you the ropes. Coach O'Neal is second in command of this raw outfit and you'll answer to him."

I look at this hickory nut of a man who seems as hard as he is short. Bracing for a string of orders from him to start doing my job, he takes me by surprise. "Don't you worry 'bout Poco, Buck, his bark's worse than his bite." Flip puts his tanned arm around my shoulder. "Let's see, your main job is to keep up with everything not nailed down—bats, equipment, rosin bags, towels and balls, especially the balls 'cause Poco goes ape when we lose a good ball."

"What about tape, bandages, merchurachrome and liniment," I ask to show him I know something about the game.

"I take care of those supplies," he says, pointing to a large black valise hanging in the dugout. "You need to come to the clubhouse 'bout a half-hour before practice to haul the bats and stuff to the field."

"I have to go to school 'til three for three more weeks. That's why Poco's mad at me right now."

"He's got a lot on his mind shaping up these greenhorns for the first game next week. Tell you what, I'll get some of the boys to help with the equipment 'til after school."

"Flip pats me on the back and changes back into a monster. "Batting practice, all up," he screams. "Steiner, you pitch. Mickler, you catch. House, Turner, Lakestraw and you in the gray cap, cover the infield. Pitchers start warming up and everybody else in the outfield. All right, let's get the lead out. Shake a leg there with that backstop."

The batter helps Poco and Flip roll the homemade backstop behind home plate. The small wheels at each of the three corners of the leadpipe and chicken wire contraption balk in the red dirt, but soon they lift it into position. Flip plops sand bags over the rear wheel to keep it from toppling over on the hitter. Poco shakes one side checking its stability. "If this heat don't kill somebody, this hillbilly chicken coup will," he grumbles. I look around to see if Mr. Holley hear the bitter words about his creation. He's nowhere in sight.

"Batter up," calls Flip. "Jake, you're it."

The player looks around, goes back to the dugout and asks, "Where're the bats?"

Flip hustles over to his black bag, digs out a string of keys tosses them to me. "Hey, Buck, run over to the clubhouse and fetch that bag of bats locked inside the equipment cage. "You boys grab a ball, pair off and limber up 'til he gets back."

I make haste past the mill office and the school to the clubhouse, but the trip back takes a while longer. The heavy bat bag takes all the muscle and wind I can manage. With the canvas bag over my shoulder, I return to Briers Field and dump the bats behind the batting cage. The field is unusually quiet and the team is gathered in the home dugout listening to the manager. I hand the keys to Flip as Poco ends his talk. "All right boys, it's late so everybody take five swings, run three laps and call it a day. Wait, before you start, I want you to know we have a batboy now, his name is Buck."

I tip my Dad's old Chiefs cap and try not to grin too big. A player throws his first baseman's pad out in the dirt. "Batboy, fetch my glove," he yells. A strange order, but with everybody watching, I rush to retrieve the glove. As I bend over, something slams against my butt nearly knocking me over. Before I can turn around a blast of gloves strike me and scatter on the ground like leaves under a cottonwood. The players howl with laughter and gather to pick up their missiles. Some add a gentle swat, "for good measure," and say something like "welcome to the team." Just as I think the initiation is over somebody sneaks up and dumps the bucket of cold water over my head. There's just enough left to soak my shirt to the skin.

"Hey, you with the bucket," the first baseman hollers, "you ruined my glove!" he reaches for the dripping wet pad in my hands. "Stupid jerk!"

"Ease up, Ike, that's the way we break in new men on the team back in Illinois."

"Then y'all can go on back to 'Illinoise'," Ike shouts sounding out the 's'. "We don't mistreat kids down here in Alabama. Anyhow, our batboy ain't no man and he don't play on the team."

The batting practice pitcher tosses the bucket and stomps away. Flip hands me a towel, "That Steiner's gonna be trouble.

Mark my word, I've seen his kind before." He takes the wet pad from Ike and shakes it. "Like Poco always says, 'Pitchers are a crazy lot.' Here, Ike, just rub a little neat's-foot oil on it and it'll be good as new."

I try to make myself useful. "I've got some neat's-foot oil at home, at least my dad does. I'll fix your glove Mr. Ike since I caused all the trouble."

"Ike, son, just call me Ike. Much obliged. Try to get it done by tomorrow so I won't have to use a regular glove at first base."

"Yessir." I hang his pad on my belt and gather the bats. As I move toward the grandstand, Peggy Sue Slater stands in my path talking to Ike Catchings. She must have watched my initiation. I duck my head and try to slip by them, but Ike catches me by the arm.

"No need for a rush job on my glove, Buck. This young lady's offered me her daddy's pad for a couple of days."

Peggy Sue lifts her chin and aims a big smile right at me. "Hi Buck, you gimme a holler if you need any help." She shows enough grace not to mention I'm wet as a hog in a puddle. I lug the bat bag to the clubhouse hoping the warm breeze will dry my clothes. It gives me time to think of how to take up Peggy Sue's offer without admitting I really want her help.

Mother and Dad greet me as I poke along up the steps to the front porch. "Sorry I got your cap wet, Dad. I hope it's not ruined."

"My goodness, did you fall in the creek, Buck?" Mother removes the cap and pushes my hair back. "Are you all right? Go inside and take off those wet clothes before the night air. . ."

"Wait a minute, I want to hear what happened," Dad insists.

"You boys think angels are looking after you no matter what!" Mother exclaims. "That's why so many jackasses wake up dead around here. I'm going in to run hot water in the tub." She lets the screen door slam behind her.

Dad chuckles, "We may as well go in and get those wet things off before she has a hissy-fit."

Mother wraps a towel around my shoulders as I tell them about my initiation as batboy. "That's a new one on me. I've heard of pounding a new preacher at church, but not a new batboy," Dad says, not bothering to hide his amusement.

"It's not funny, J. D. Giving our preacher a pound of this and a pound of that is a whole lot different and you know it. Buck could wind up with pneumonia."

While Mother and Dad fuss over whether I will live or die, I realize Ike's wet glove is missing. I search my damp clothes on the floor.

"What are you looking for?"

"The pad, Ike's pad, I must have dropped it. I'd better go find it or he'll kill me."

"You mean that soggy ol' thing?" Mother points to the floor. "I laid it beside the stove to dry off."

"I promised to work in some neat's-foot oil before it ruins. Dad, can I use some of yours?"

"O. K., but not 'til the leather is nearly dry. Oil and water don't mix."

After my bath, Dad shows me how to work water out of the glove with a dry towel before applying the oil. He opens the bottle and sniffs the oil as though it contains an elixir that drums up faded memories of the Chiefs. "How did practice go today aside from the drenching?"

"I didn't have time to watch and keep up with my job."

"You got along with Poco and everybody?"

"I guess so, except there's one feller I won't ever like, that short bald Yankee pitcher who wet me down."

"Sounds like Squat Steiner. He'll be all right. You may change your mind after getting to know him better. Reminds me of the time when I first met Frog McGee. I was new on the job in the spinning room and he was supposed to show me how to doff a frame, taking full spools of thread off and putting empty bobbins on. After a week, I found out he had me doffing his frames and mine too. Boy, was I hot. It took me a while, but I got over it to the point that we both could laugh about it."

Dad hands me Ike's pad to finish. "That reminds me, son. First chance you get, take Frog's bat back to the team where it belongs."

I stop rubbing oil into the glove and close my eyes to block out Dad's order. One more bat in the bag is all I need to cave in my back. But that's not my biggest worry. I don't want the burden of dealing with a bat possessed by the spirit of a dead hind-catcher.

Chapter 6

Carl Craig's stories in the *River Bend Lookout* help town folk work up a head of steam to give the new Millers a grand sendoff on opening day at Briers Field. He calls the team, "Our town's gateway to professional baseball." Some men arrive early, tap their fingers on the glossy green benches, making sure the paint is dry and then settle their wives and children into choice seats in the grandstand. Leaving their broods to hold the seats, the men wander around to inspect the refurbished home of the Millers. They tug at the shiny chicken wire protective screen and read the names painted on the box seats to see who shelled out enough money to afford special season passes. There are no surprises. Fuzzy Wetzel, Coley Farmer and Paul Anderson own front row center boxes. In the box near the home dugout, two slatted chairs stand empty. The name *McGee* is stenciled on the back.

"You gonna dress out today, J. D.?" Mayor Robbins pushes his way past players in front of the dugout and slaps Dad on the back. "Need a good man on third today," he says laughing.

"Naw, I think Ted Rich here can handle that hot corner without my help. Besides who'd keep score?" Dad tries to wangle the starting line-up from Poco while the team crowds around to see who starts the game.

"Hey there, Poco, I need to borrow Snuffy Veasey and a ball," the Mayor says. Poco shoots a cold look at the Mayor, but says nothing. "I gotta warm-up before I throw out the first pitch." Snuffy grabs his mitt, fishes a ball out of the bag at Poco's feet and leads Robbins toward right field. Poco mumbles something about not needing to warm-up just to throw out the first pitch.

Poco presses a tack through the batting order card and sticks it on the dugout wall. The players push forward to look for their names. Stretch Slagle gets closest, so he calls out the starters' names, "Davis, Rich, Colbert, Glover and Catchings." He swallows hard before going on because he and Ike both play first base, "Lakestraw and Strong. Battery is Mickler catching and King pitching." After some groaning and back-patting, the fresh Miller starters hustle to their positions popping their gloves.

Flip grabs the outfield fungo and tells me to follow him with a couple of balls. Poco shoves a new ball in his back pocket, picks up the shorter fungo and heads to home plate. "C'mon boys, hustle up. We've gotta get done before the cer-eee-monies begin." Mr. Holley and another man in coveralls move a knee-high platform out behind home plate and stand until Poco notices them. Disgusted, Poco calls a halt to infield practice and waves the team off the field. After setting the platform over home plate, Mr. Holley places a microphone stand on the front edge.

"Testing, testing, one, two, three, testing," Mr. Craig speaks into the mike and taps it several times. The buzz of the gathering fans diminishes as the newspaper editor prepares to welcome them to opening day. Suddenly, a popping noise like firecrackers draws everyone's attention to the maintenance gate near the right field fence. A motor scooter with no muffler putters down the foul line. Long poles with banners flying in its wake stick out from each side. As the loud two-wheeler approaches, its driver begins shouting something I cannot make out. The scooter veers toward a group of Millers gathered between first base and the dugout. Flip recognizes Fuzzy Wetzel has lost control of his mount and begins pushing players out of his path. In his haste, Flip fails to notice a loose bat left on the ground. I run to kick the bat out of Fuzzy's route, but too late. The front wheel pops over the bat causing the scooter to veer toward the platform where Mr. Craig freezes in disbelief. The two-wheeler hits the make-shift stage, bumps away and sputters until it flounders taking Fuzzy with it to the ground. Unfazed, he picks up his spectacles, dusts off his red blazer and yells, "Go get 'em Millers." The crowd's gasps turn into a roar of relief.

As I retrieve the bat, Poco fusses, "Dammit, boy. You've gotta keep up with them bats. That idiot, I mean, Mr. Wetzel could've been banged up and crashed our season as well. Now get that broke bat outta the way." A close look at the bat shows me it didn't break, not even a scratch on it. It's Frog McGee's bat, the crazy one. I'm sure I left it in the bag by the dugout. I never took it out even for batting practice. How did it wind up in Mr. Wetzel's path? I decide to line it up with the rest of the bats and turn away.

"Buck, Buck," a deep coarse voice whispers, then laughs. I jerk around and see only a row of bats in the dirt. The kids sitting on top of the dugout pay me no mind. I shake my head and direct my attention to Mr. Craig rearranging the microphone on the platform. Fuzzy continues to brush the dusts and lime off his coat and pants. I think about a perfect game today, the batboy makes no errors.

After a few speeches by the big mules, promised to be short but delivered long, Mr. Craig introduces the players on the opposing team, "All the way from Griffin, Georgia. They tip their gray and orange road caps and form a line from home plate to third base. A chorus of "boo's" overpower the cheers from a pod of fans sitting near the opponents' dugout. Although Mr. Craig chides our fans for not being good sports, they drown him out with Bronx cheers.

"And now it is my distinct pleasure to introduce the brand new River Bend Millers, a name submitted by Tad McGee, son of the Cherokee Chiefs great hind-catcher, Frog McGee. Stand and take a bow, Tad." The fans cheer, whistle and clap, but they search for Tad in vain. I look at his reserved box seat, but no Tad. It's Peggy Sue Slater sitting with Tad's mother. She waves her first base pad, but I pretend not to notice.

As Carl Craig introduces each Miller and says a bit about his background, my mind wanders back a week ago to Poco's dilemma and his worry about filling the team roster with five more players.

~~~~

"I'm not as worried about field positions as I am about two more pitchers," he says to Carl Craig who dropped by practice looking for a story. "I need a lefty but I'll take anybody who can find home plate at this stage."

"Did you contact some of the former Cherokee Chiefs?" Mr. Craig asks.

"Not directly, but I tacked up notices in the pool room and bowling alley. Nothing's come of them."

"O. K. that'll be my lead this week. Maybe some hibernating Steamboat Johnson will read my column and come running out of the cotton patch before opening day next week.

"Thanks Carl, I appreciate your effort." He salutes and walks to the infield. Mr. Craig stops by while I mark off the on-deck circle with dry lime.

"I heard about you and your dad helping out with the team, Buck. It'll be like old times sitting with him in the press box along with Bull Ingram."
~~~~

"Bull, the disk jockey?"

"Yes, Bull's going to announce the home games when he can get away from the station. He'll do a good. . ."

Bang! A foul ball hits the tin roof. "Gotta go sir, that's my call." I bound up the grandstand two rows at a time as I had a dozen times before and run out the main gate smack into a wall of denim. I brace my self against the door to keep my balance. "Sorry, mister, I didn't see you."

The rangy stranger laughs and hands me a baseball. His overalls and gray-blue shirt are covered with lint. The smell of denim dye, sweat and chewing tobacco tell me he's a mill hand fresh from his shift. He pulls a trainman's striped cap off his head, wipes his forehead with his sleeve and says, "Betcha looking for this." His fingers wrap around the ball almost hiding it from view.

"Thanks, mister; I was just coming to fetch it."

"If you wanna oblige me with a favor, boy, can you point out Mr. Poco to me?"

"That's him standing by first base with his hands in his back pockets. But don't call him Mister, he likes just plain Poco."

I follow the gangly mill hand down the steps. His gait is like a marionette being guided along by a set of imaginary strings. He removes a folded dishrag of a glove from his hip pocket and slaps it against his overalls with a puff of lint trailing behind. He stops, looks back at me and gestures towards Poco. I nod and he makes his way toward first base. A brief word with the manager and he retraces his steps in my direction shaking his head.

The man stops in his tracks at the sound of Poco's booming voice. "Hold on there Parker, I've decided to let you show me what you can do." Poco waves Benny Lane off the mound, takes the ball and waves the stranger forward like a relief pitcher. "Batboy, fetch Jake Colbert a bat." I meet Jake at home plate as Poco barks out instructions. "We're gonna see how this. . ." Poco removes his cap, looks back to the mound and wipes his forearm across his eyes as in disbelief, ". . .how this gentleman pitches." Jake, so far the team's best batter had come to River Bend with Poco and Flip. He can hit any pitch near the plate, but he labors over running because one leg is slightly shorter than the other. "Stand in and hit only what he throws across the plate," Poco advises Jake and takes his position behind the batting cage to watch.

"What's your name, buddy?" Jake asks the stranger.

"They call me Alfred Parker, what's yours?"

"Jake Colbert."

"All right Mr. Jake, tell me when you're ready."

"Waiting on you Mr. Alfred," Jake says with a grin, glancing at Poco as he steps into the batter's box.

Without a windup, Parker hunches over, cocks his arm much like a softball pitcher and let's the ball fly sidearm. It shoots over the batting cage like a cannonball and bangs against the grandstand eave. "My fault," the pitcher says to Jake and then points to Poco, "My fault, sir, my fault, I gotta fix this rut in front of this rubber thing. It made me slip."

Jake backs away from home plate shaking his head. Poco screws up his face and picks up the stray ball at his feet looking for any damage that might set him off. After Parker tamps down the mound with his work shoes, Poco tosses the ball back to him. Parker leans over and fires one directly over the plate. Jake, standing farther away from the plate, lets it go by for safety's sake.

At Poco's bid, I rush out to the mound and lay a half dozen practice balls at Parker's feet. Jake lets one more perfect strike go by before taking a swing. He lines the next three pitches deep into left field.

"Parker, can you throw anything besides that looping underhanded pitch?" yells Poco.

"Not iffen y'all want 'im to hit it."

"For crying out loud, son, I've seen him hit. I wanna see if you can throw a pitch by him," stammers Poco. "Strike 'im out."

"Oh, that's different."

Without changing his approach, Parker throws every pitch except a knuckle ball; curve balls, fast balls and one with a funny twitch at the plate. Jake swings at six or seven pitches and gets a piece of only one, a dribble foul down third base line.

Jake tosses the bat to the ground in mock disgust and walks out to shake Alfred Parker's hand. "Mr. Alfred, you're one pitcher I hope never to face in a game."

"My mama calls me Alfred. Everybody at work calls me 'Scoopy'," he flashes a big toothy grin.

Poco, joining the two at the mound, asks, "Parker, where did you play baseball?"

"Ain't played much, 'cept a few cow pasture games out where I live, but the fellas I played with didn't let me pitch much."

"I can see why," Jake says.

"You show up tomorrow at two and we'll see if we can find a spot for you on the squad."

"Can't hardly oblige, Mr. Poco."

"Didn't you come to tryout just now?"

"Yessir, but I don't get off work 'til two."

Poco glances at me and shakes his head. "I see. All right, show up when you can. Buck here will find you a decent glove. By the way, drop the 'mister', there aren't any misters on this team, including me."

Watching his new pitcher walk away, Poco mumbles something about putting up with crazy pitchers. "Flip, find Scoopy a uniform before opening day next week and make him take a shower before he puts it on." Poco waves his hand in front of his nose.

~~~~

Mr. Craig drags out the introduction of the Millers. Most had played for cotton mill teams in nearby towns, but some are experienced minor leaguers. Jake Colbert and Marty Davis came with Poco to River Bend. Little else is known about the trio except for four Louisville Sluggers engraved with Poco Walker's signature, the favorite bats of both players.

As Digger Dugan is introduced, he fakes a pronounced limp to take his place on the first base line. His clowning around never stops. This joker barely made the team last week with only four practice days left. I remember refilling the water bucket from the spigot behind the visiting team's dugout and Poco said, "Buck, hustle out and tell Flip to meet me in the dugout."
~~~~

Poco and Flip huddle in the dugout in secrecy. Flip walks out, pretends to straighten the line of bats on the ground and glances intently at the grandstand. He goes back to confer with Poco.

"Hey, Buck," Flip invites me to join their confab.

"Don't look now, but do you know that stranger sitting in the grandstand behind the girl?"

I pick up a bat, pretend to swing it and focus on two figures in the seats. "I don't know the man, but that's Peggy Sue Slater sitting in front of him."

"This is the third day he's spied on us," Flip says, "Go tell him I want to talk to him."

Peggy Sue grins real big as I walk toward her. She's shown up at every practice and helped shag foul balls hit over the grandstand. The stranger rises to his feet behind her and spreads a smile across his face showing large protruding teeth that shine like corn on the cob. His jutting lower jaw makes his face long like a thoroughbred racehorse. Tan smooth skin stretches over a sea of rippling muscles on his arms. "Howdy, boy," he seems to know my mission. "Y'all coming after me?" Peggy Sue pouts at being ignored.

"Coach wants to see you." I start to call him "mister" but he's nearly my age.

"Much obliged," he says and trots out to the field.

Peggy Sue tugs at my shirt, "Ask Poco if he needs another first baseman." She giggles and waves her Dad's pad.

"You're not a man, yet, I mean you're still a girl, I mean. . ."

"Glad you noticed," she says with a teasing grin and pops her fist into the pad. "Mama said I can't watch the games from the dugout roof anymore. Can you guess why she told me that?" I am speechless. "Because it's not lady-like," Peggy Sue says releasing her grip on my shirt. "Mama's afraid you'll see my drawers and forget what you're supposed to do." That's what I'm thinking, but don't care for her blasting it out to the whole world.

"Hey son, you scouting our team?" Flip hollers to the stranger.

"Naw, I heard y'all looking for a pitcher."

"You gotta name, boy?"

"Digger, Digger Dugan from over in Ourtown."

"Ever play ball?"

"A couple-a years in high school 'fore I quit and went to work."

"Work, where?"

"In the company warehouse." Digger throws one arm in the air but not towards Cherokee Mill. That explains the muscles, moving 500 pound bales of cotton around using only hand trucks.

"I'm afraid the team has too many mill hands. Their shifts interfere with practice. Anyhow, I'm looking for more experienced pitchers right now." Flip waves him off with his hand.

"Oh, I work on the night shift Mayfair mill 'cross town. Making practice ain't no hassle with me." Flip cocks his head to listen further. "The notice says y'all want a hook-arm pitcher, so I come to watch practice a few times before trying out."

Flip tells me, “Buck, take this fella over to do some wind sprints with the other pitchers. I’ll check out his delivery at batting practice.”

Poco lines up his five pitchers in center field to sprint to the right field foul line. He holds up while I introduce Digger Dugan. With stop watch in hand, Poco yells “Go” and Digger outruns the others by four or five paces. Squat Steiner takes up the challenge. “That was only a trot for us, this time it’ll be a race.”

The pitchers line up again and Digger wins again, this time by two paces. Not satisfied, Squat removes his warm-up jacket and insists on a rematch with just him and the rookie. Digger takes off his heavy brogans and whizzes across the line leaving Squat in his wake. Poco yells to the rest of the team that had gathered to watch the race, “Now, ladies, that’s how you’re supposed to run.” He rooster trots over to Digger and pats him on the back. “Boys, this is Digger Dugan. He’s come to try out for the team, so let’s see what he can do on the mound.”

Digger’s tryout is a disaster. His hard fast balls rarely find the plate but he makes the team under one condition. “I’ll give you ten days to control your pitches. The first batter you bean puts you off the team,” Poco warns. “Anybody who runs that fast and throws with heat can help the team if he learns how to pitch strikes.”

~~~~

Mr. Craig continues presenting River Bend’s roster of players:

Pitchers—Speed King, Digger Dugan, Benny Lane, Squat Steiner and Scoopy Parker;
~~~~

Hind-catchers—Red Mickler and Snuffy Veasey;

Infielders—Ike Catchings, Stretch Slagle, Jackie House, Marty Davis and Ted Rich;

Outfielders—Jake Colbert, Bo Turner and Jimmy Glover.

Utility fielders—Phil Lakestraw and Willie Strong.

"And finally, our distinguished veteran of the St. Louis Browns, Oregon native, Manager Poco Walker."

Thinking the introductions are over, the Griffin Pimentoes Manager strolls towards home plate with roster in hand, but Fuzzy Wetzel grabs the microphone stopping the anxious manager in his cleats.

The Millers, green and unseasoned in their fresh white uniforms trimmed in cardinal red, stop popping fists in their gloves and the umpires back away from the platform. Amid some tedious moans from the grandstand, Fuzzy prolongs the ceremonies with a promise not to take long, but, "Before Mayor Robbins throws out the first pitch, I've got two more presentations to make." Digger Dugan amuses the fans with a grossly exaggerated yawn behind Fuzzy's back. "What's a team without a coach? Will Mr. Flip O'Neal step up front and center."

Flip approaches the platform and accepts a red jacket the color of his face from Fuzzy. As Flip slips on the jacket with the letters C-O-A-C-H stiched on the back, Carl Craig hands Fuzzy another one. "And what's a professional team without a batboy? Buck Clinton, son of that great Chiefs third baseman and now the Millers scorekeeper, J. D. Clinton, come on up here so you can become properly dressed out."

After putting on the jacket with B-A-T-B-O-Y spread across the back, I do not remember seeing the Mayor's first pitch, or the ump yelling, “Play ball,” and by the time the Millers come up to bat, I’m still admiring my new warm-up jacket and watching Peggy Sue wave her first base pad at me.

I snap into my batboy role and hand Marty Davis a bat. Again I hear that mysterious coarse voice whispering, “Atta boy, Buck, atta boy.”

Marty tugs at the bat. “C’mon Buck, wake up and let go the bat unless you wanna lead off the inning.”

He takes the bat and picks up another one, swings both inside the on-deck circle while the Pimentos pitcher finishes his warm-up tosses. He discards one of the bats and takes a stance in the batters box. Marty smashes the first pitch into deep right-center for a triple to start the bottom half of the first inning. When I retrieve his bat I make a shocking discovery. He had hit that triple with Frog McGee’s old bat, the crazy one.

Chapter 7

His transition from third baseman to team scorekeeper is a harsh adjustment for Dad. His image of baseball begins to fade around the edges. When I was a little kid, he'd let me go with him to the dressing room. While he showered and changed into street clothes, I'd listen to the players bragging about winning or griping about losing the game. Either way it was genuine baseball talk. Now, instead of jawboning with players, he rushes home to call in the batteries, box scores and such to the *Birmingham Post.* It seems all the flavor has been sucked out of the whole nine innings. Mother complains, "Do y'all have to bring all that baseball talk inside my house? Why don't you leave it in the clubhouse like before?"

Dad's answer is simple, "If I do that, then we won't need this telephone the club's paying for. Finally, Mother gives in. She'll put up with baseball talk rather than give up the only telephone she's ever had. I think she admires Dad's little contributions to the daily sports page but doesn't show it.

Reporting game results wears thin for Dad after the first two games of the season. Griffin stomps the Millers. First it was 9-0 and the second game was worse, 14-zip. After the Pimentos score ten runs and our team comes up to bat in the bottom of the fourth inning, Poco Walker announces, "You guys sit tight after the game if it ever gets over. Snuffy, you coach at first and Flip, you take my place at third. Poco retreats to a bench to tough out the rest of the game without watching it. He tries to fade into the woodwork of the dugout.

Our boys do all right from then on, letting Griffin score only four more runs. After the final out, the chief umpire delivers the game balls to Poco along with a pay voucher. Poco signs the voucher and inspects each ball for marks and scrapes. While the players jostle for seats in the dugout. Poco stumbles across the line of bats on the ground and curses me, "Hell batboy, get these damn bats outta my way and take 'em on to the clubhouse. You don't need to hear this."

Flip helps me dump the bats into the new bag made of heavy mill cloth. He gives me the clubhouse keys and I make my way through the spatter of fans lingering in the grandstand. Poco's tirade starts before I leave the field. Dad will surely tell me the cleaned up version later.

Dad and I arrive at home at the same time. After he hangs up the phone, he closes the scorebook and heads off my questions. "Poco cussed out the team, son, with words not fit for your ears. I haven't heard such foul talk from any man since basic training. But, I can repeat something he called the players—lollygaggers, which the army called goldbricking. Poco threatened to make the players wear skirts and carry bushel baskets instead of gloves at the next game."

"What for?"

"To trap the balls they missed," Dad chuckles. "He should've known the boys are green, something a little experience will cure. Like when Marty Davis hit that home run, he was so excited he forgot to touch second base."

"You mean that run didn't count?"

"No, the boy left it on the scoreboard by mistake. He's a little green too. That's all you need to know about the meeting except Poco cancelled their day off this Thursday."

"I reckon I'd better be there."

"Yeah, and I hope they come back from LaGrange with a win under their belts or it will be a long hard practice."

"There's something I need to tell you, Dad."

"I know what you're gonna say, the answer is 'no'. You can't go on the road trip to LaGrange."

"I know. It's about Mr. McGee's funny bat."

"Is it acting up again?"

"Didn't you just tell the sports editor that Marty Davis is the star hitter on the team?"

"That's right, he's hit five for seven in two games. The home run didn't count and he walked once. What does he have to do with the bat?"

"In the opening game, he picked up the crazy bat by mistake and hit a triple. Next time up when I gave him his bat, he asked for the long one, Mr. McGee's. He's gone to bat with it ever since and now he claims it as his own. He tells me not to let anyone else touch his bat."

"So, Marty chose Frog's bat."

"No sir-ee. That bat chose Marty. That's what I think."

Dad opens the scorebook and checks out Marty's at-bats. "Let's see, two triples, a double, a pop foul, two singles, a walk and a home-run called out. This is mighty strange. He doesn't hit like a lead-off man or a short-stop. He closes the book and divides five by seven. "Humm, a .714 average. Nobody hits that good, especially an infielder. Well, son, we'll just have to wait and see what happens on the road."

"How will we find out? Are you going along?"

No, son, other teams have their own scorekeepers. We'll read box scores in the paper like everyone else."

Quite a crowd shows up to witness the unscheduled team practice on Thursday. Fuzzy Wetzel tries to pump up the players who are dragging their chins in the dirt. Dad and Carl Craig review the score sheets from the two losses to LaGrange. The usual covey of high school girls tries to catch the eyes of uniformed single men from their nest in a box seat behind home plate. Peggy Sue shows up to help chase down stray foul balls. Off-shift mill hands and town-folks seem starved for more baseball as they anchor their butts to the shiny new grandstand bench seats.

Poco shows no mercy as he puts the team through a workout from the backside of hades. To begin, he hits infield practice so hard the players inch backwards onto the outfield grass. "Com'on you pansies, charge the ball. Get your aprons down. Nothing gets through, nothing. Wish them girls would go on home," he mutters and spits a glob of brown that punches up a tiny spray of dust. He drives a worm-burner to Ted Rich knocking him backward as he stops it between his legs. "Atta-boy, nothing gets through."

When Squat and Digger drift over and chat with the girls, Poco orders them to take ten laps around the field. The grueling session goes on past sundown. While sacking the bats, I overhear Squat grumbling about too much work for such lousy pay. "Do y'all get paid for playing baseball?" I ask.

"Are you kidding? There's no way I'd put up with Poco's torture without a paycheck at the end of the month, as little as it is."

While I'm trying to figure out why men actually take money for playing baseball, Marty taps me on the shoulder. "Have you seen my bat, Buck?" I check each one in the bag and shake my head. "It wasn't in the bag at LaGrange, shot my average to hell."

I heft the full bag of bats to my shoulder and start the long walk back to the clubhouse. "Wait a sec, Buck," Flip calls from the dugout. "Don't forget this one." He pulls a bat from behind the bench and lobs it toward me. It hits the ground at my feet with a thud. Its trademark face stares at me.

Marty whips around me and exclaims, "What?" Wild eyed, he repeats, "What? Buck what did you say?"

I shake my head, still transfixed by the face on Frog's bat. Marty picks up the bat. "I'll be damned, if that don't beat all. Where'd you find it?" He slides the bat between his legs to clean the dust off. "Thanks, Buck. I'll hang on to my bat until the game tomorrow, not letting this baby out of my sight again."

Dad and I trail behind the weary players to the clubhouse. The street lights come on adding a bit of spookiness to the end of the day. I can tell by his questions he thinks I had something to do with the missing crazy bat. "I hate to sound superstitious, but Frog's old bat, well, it didn't sprout legs and walk into the dugout by itself. Somebody's throwing you a curve ball, do you think?"

I have nothing else to say. Dad doesn't know how much I hate to touch that weird piece of hardwood with the face that smiles at me and nobody else.

Disappointment hangs over the dressing room like boiler room smoke over the village on a cloudy day. The players grab a quick shower and dress to escape before Poco can spew any left over venom on them. Coley Farmer tries to cheer up the players as they hurry out the door. He and Dad are the only "civilians" allowed in the dressing room since he pays the bills.

“Four in a row,” he says before Poco stows the bag of balls in his oversize locker. “At least we got some runs.” Poco strips and heads for the now empty shower room ignoring Coley. “Man, I like the smell of a locker room; the liniment, wintergreen, Lifebuoy; reminds me of high school football.” He fails to mention the reeking mixture of sweat and foot dip. Flip jokes about how the aroma of tar from the dip drives pretty girls crazy.

Poco emerges from the shower and finds Coley still talking to himself. I toss the weary manager a towel. He covers his head, rubbing it briskly as if to erase Coley from his presence. Spreading the towel on the bench, Poco sits on it and fans Coley’s cigar smoke away from his face.

“Fuzzy and I drove down to LaGrange yesterday and caught the last few innings of the game.”

Poco looks puzzled. “Oh?”

“Yeah, since the whole town closes up on Wednesday afternoons, we sneaked away. Got there just in time to see Digger steal second and third before scoring on Ike’s fly ball.” No response from Poco. “That Digger runs like a rabbit. When do you think he’ll be ready to pitch instead of pinch running?”

From the gritting of Poco’s teeth, Coley realizes he has crossed the line into the manager’s domain. “Remember Mr. Farmer, I manage the team and you manage the money.”

“There’s no rain in the forecast for tomorrow’s game with Opelika,” Coley says returning to a safer subject.

The last player in the room pauses before the mirror runs a comb through his wet hair and leaves. Dad follows him out the door.

Poco tells me to go help Flip with the laundry. He obviously wants to be left alone with Coley Farmer.

I pile the gray road uniforms and damp towels into the laundry bags. Flip turns off the fan so he can hear the discussion growing louder by the minute. "Payday's coming up and gate receipts won't cover the payout," Coley's voice echoes from the locker room, "Those boys ate up our club's cut of the Lagrange ticket sales."

"They probably gave out a lot of free tickets to draw a crowd like we did. That's what made our take come up short at LaGrange. I think you ought to take up your complaint with the boys at LaGrange instead of me," Poco says.

"That won't be easy. The Atlanta Crackers own that farm club and it won't be easy dealing with their front office."

"Well, I ain't gonna run a club that starves its players on the road and that's that!" A brief silence. "Anything else on your mind Mr. Treasurer?"

"One more thing, those Trailways busses cost too much, so Cherokee Mill offers to lend us their bus for some of our road trips this summer," Coley says.

"That tired old Reo? What if it breaks down on the road and we have to forfeit some games? That'll cost more than a chartered bus."

Watching Poco guard new baseballs like precious jewels adds to my already jaded image of baseball as a mere game. Last year, when the team needed new balls the mill supplied 'em. All this talk about making money tires me out. I stack the stuffed laundry bags in a bin outside to be picked up and leave the two men to hammer out their differences. Flip follows me out to get a breath of fresh air.

"It gets warm earlier here than in Bend," Flip says wiping sweat from his face."

"You mean River Bend?"

"No, Bend, a little town tucked in a corner of Oregon where Poco managed a team before the war. We could stand on the street and see snow in the Cascades this time of year."

"Wow, why did y'all leave, didn't you like it there?"

"It's quite simple, Poco returned from combat ready to swap his major's uniform for his old baseball outfit, but there were no teams left to manage. We spent the winter hanging around major league training camps in Arizona until Poco heard about this new league starting up so we rounded up a couple of stray players and hopped a train bound for River Bend."

"That was quick."

"Yep, Poco exchanged telegrams with Mr. Wetzel and we were on our way to the South."

Coley Farmer leaves the dressing room, climbs into his Packard and roars off into the moonless night.

"He's blowing off steam through his tail pipe," quips Flip.

"Why does Mr. Farmer hang out in the dressing room so much? He seems to come in joking around and leave mad."

"It's this funny business of baseball that gets him and Poco in a twit. Coley deals with money everyday as a banker but mixing business with his favorite sport turns him inside out."

"It's hard to believe what Steiner told me today. He gets paid for playing baseball."

Flip laughs and presses his fist against my shoulder faking a punch. "Surely you didn't, how do you say it 'round these parts, 'you didn't fall off no turnip greens wagon?' You don't think these boys came to this cotton mill town for their health, do you?"

Totally embarrassed, I'd like to find a hole and crawl in it. Baseball is as big as the Statue of Liberty and everyday someone chips away at my idol. Sensing my uneasiness, Flip says, "Hold on, I just remembered. You are right on the money about some members of the team. The mill hands will get a share of the profits if there's some left over at the end of the season. And Phil, Jimmy and Willie don't take money to protect their amateur status in case they go to college next year. So there you have it Buck, a part of your dream still exists."

I force a smile. "Now I see why Mr. Farmer's such a worry wart."

"Yeah, he's a watch dog for the investors."

"Investors?'

Yeah, Coley and Fuzzy put up some money to get the team started, but I'm not sure who the others are."

"I'll bet it's Mr. Craig and Mr. Alexander."

"Good thinking, you're right on the money, to coin a phrase." Flip cackles at his choice of words. "Seems to me those gentlemen's appetites for baseball are much larger than their pocket books. Now, they have to put up more money or fold the team."

"You mean quit before we get a running start?"

"My guess is they love the game enough to come up with the cash. We'll have to wait and see."

Poco comes out of the dressing room tossing his jacket over his shoulder. "Are you ready to lock up, Coach?"

Flip pats his pockets and feels the top of his head. "Lemme get my keys and hat, be right back."

I ask Poco, "Do you like living here better'n in Bend?"

He jerks his head around as if I had said a cuss word. "You mean River Bend, don't you, Buck?"

"No sir, I mean where you and Flip are from, Bend."

"Best you forget about where people come from and deal with the here and now," he warns with a stern voice. Then he changes his mood. "You're doing a right tolerable job, losing only a couple balls so far. That's pretty good."

"Yessir, one didn't make it back from LaGrange and the other one got ruined when Marty's homer landed in the creek behind right field."

Flip locks the door behind him and offers me a ride home.

"I can get there quicker by walking. Thank you."

Flip's pre-war Plymouth churns up dust as it passes under a street light. The walk home gives me time to ponder the business of baseball. I long for the good ol' days of sitting on top of the dugout and hollering for a team that enjoys playing baseball just for the fun of it.

Chapter 8

The rattling Reo bus lumbers to a stop in front of the Millers' dressing room. Troy Jolly swings open the door and untangles his long legs from under the steering wheel. "Is the team ready to go?" he asks pressing the reluctant door all the way open.

"Yessir, they're packing their gear. I wanna get these bats in the back before they load up."

"You making the trip with the team, Buck?"

"Wish I could, but Dad says I can't go without him. He doesn't go on road trips. Anyway he's at work."

"Tell you what, Buck. After you stick the bats in back, run home and tell your mama that I'm driving the bus and I'll see after you if she'll let you go to Sylacauga with the team." His words are hardly out of his mouth as I stow the bats away and hit the ground running home. Surely Mother will let me go with my scoutmaster.

"Mother's still asleep and you'd better not wake her up," whispers Bobbie Jean sitting with Annie on the edge of the porch blocking my way.

"Get outta my way, she didn't work last night."

"She got up early and did the wash and now she's resting."

Waking Mother would guarantee a "no" answer. I bounce down the steps to report the let down to Mr. Jolly. On the way back I stop at mill gate number two and say howdy to a mill hand taking a smoke break.

"Do you know my Dad, J. D. Clinton? He works in the spinning room."

"Yep, he's just inside this door about two frames over. You want me to fetch him?"

The lint-flecked older man steps inside and waves his arm. Soon Dad appears in the doorway. "What's the matter, Buck. Is your mother sick? Are the girls all right?"

Embarrassed there's no crisis, I blurt out my plea, "Can I go with the team to Sylacauga? Mr. Jolly said he'll look after me."

"Go ask your mother,"

"She's asleep."

"I gotta get back to work." He hesitates and gives in. "Go ahead. Here's a quarter to get something to eat." Pressing the coin in my hand he adds, "Make sure Poco O. K.'s you to go."

"Betcha britches, sir."

The old Reo bustles with players who've been together long enough to kid around poking fun at each other. They team up much better off the field than in a game. A string of more losses than wins doesn't seem to dampen their spirits. Marty Davis, their best hitter, does his part by getting on base thanks to this adopted bat, but he's stranded on base most the time. Poco preaches teamwork every chance he gets, but Flip shakes his head, "Having one or two more sluggers would help a lot." I think about suggesting that Marty share his bat with another player, but decide against wandering into that unknown rabbit hole.

Flip greets me smiling, "Troy said you might come along so I packed your jacket and shirt in my bag." I am surprised that he allows my zero-number shirt and jacket space inside his guarded bag that most players call "Coach's giant purse." He always unzips his bag hunched over guarding its contents like Poco protects the baseballs. No matter, I'm glad to be his batboy and his buddy.

The overcrowded Reo provokes a bit of grousing inside. "We'd have more room if we had some place to put our gear," Digger complains.

"Just pretend your bag's that girl I see you with. Hold her in your lap and hug her tight," Marty quips.

"Like you hug that old bat, huh Marty," Digger snaps. "It ain't human you know." Like Flip and his black bag, Marty's never seen without his favorite bat. With all seats filled, I sit on the bat bag in back and brace for the half-hour ride to my first game away from Briers Field.

Snuffy Veasy offers me a cookie but Digger's big hand forges into the paper bag ahead of mine. Snuffy jumps up, grabs Digger's hand and snatches the cookie out of his grip. "If that don't beat all, stealing a kid's cookie."

"Crap, Shorty, just funning the kid. Don't get your skivvies in a wad." Digger jerks Snuffy's cap down over his eyes and cackles through his rabbit-like teeth. Digger manages to get under everybody's skin, but it's hard not to like him. His base running helped win two games. Parker's fast ball won the other two.

"I'll make you a deal, Digger," says Phil King.

"What's that Mr. slow-ball pitcher?"

"If you steal at least three bases today, I'll bake you a dozen cookies myself."

"That ain't no deal, darlin', I'd as soon eat pig slop as somethin' you'd fix." Digger laughs hard at his own jab.

Snuffy swallows his pride and offers a different deal. "Look, Digger, we've got to have some runs today. If you steal those bases, I'll get Maxine to bake you a whole sack full of these sugar cookies for our next road trip."

"You tell that purty li'l wife of your'n that I'd steal every base in Sylacauga for some o' her cookin'."

Troy turns on the windshield wipers and the players moan in unison. "Maybe it's not raining in Sylacauga," yells Flip trying to keep up their spirits. He adds under his breath, "We really must play this game for the sake of morale not to mention meeting this month's payroll."

We pass the city limits sign and cruise down a broad shaded lane through the center of town. The bus rumbles across double railroad tracks and the scenery changes. Troy guides the Reo along a huge brick mill with its towering smokestack and into a village of houses all in a row much like my own except these are white instead of brown. At the village edge we top a hill and the grandstand roof seems to rise from the dirt road ahead. It wears a dark green coat like Briers Field and a fresh WARRIOR PARK sign crowns the red metal roof. The field nestles at the bottom of a giant pit cut into the red clay banks protruding above the outfield fence, a batboy's heaven. Balls hit out of the park, fair or foul, would roll back against the fence for easy pickings.

Troy aims the bus toward a narrow gravel drive on the rim of the right field embankment. On past the field the bus squeals to a halt behind a warehouse. Before opening the door, Troy announces, "Y'all can dress out through that door there, but take the steps down to the field. That bank is so steep you could slide right on past first base if you slip."

"Look at that infield, boys," Flip says, "dry as grandma's talcum."

"And Scoopy's snuff box," adds Digger.

"Batting practice in fifteen minutes, boys. Get them uniforms on and let's hustle." Troy leads the group up a ramp and through one of the steel double doors into a cavernous warehouse with four rows of unsteady faded lockers. A half dozen naked light bulbs hang too high to give much light. Two giant fans spin at the ends of the building providing lots of air and only meager light from the cloudy day. The Warriors are dressed and click their spikes on the concrete floor heading out to the field.

Poco shakes hands with the Warriors' manager, a much shorter and rounder man of the same age. The two managers face each other and their potbellies form a letter "S" in profile. Thunder interrupts their talk. "What say we skip batting practice, do a short infield and get the game in before it rains," Poco suggests.

"You got it, pal."

Poco claps his hands, "All right get a move on, boys. It's time to hit the field."

I hurry to unload the bats from the bus. Troy points toward the field and says, "I put the bat bag over there by the steps. I have to take the bus and put some more air in this rear tire." A black Ford pulls in behind the Reo. Troy tells the driver to move his car so he can back the bus out.

Ignoring Troy, the man gets out, brushes dust off his black suit and touches the brim of his matching hat. After removing the sunglasses he doesn't need, he cranes his neck to scan the empty bus. "Got a game today?" he asks in a clipped accent the same as Poco Walker's.

"Yes, sir, you can buy a ticket over at that window," Troy points to the grandstand. "And you can park on the other side of this warehouse."

I start to leave, but the stranger grabs my arm. "Hold on, kid, I want to ask you some questions."

Troy jerks the man's hand away. "Mister, if you've got business here, take it up with me. Go on Buck and get your bats." I walk toward the bag, but not too fast to miss what they say.

"Where's this Miller baseball team at?" the man asks. "I need to see Marvin. Where's he at?"

"There's no Marvin on our team, maybe he plays for Sylacauga." Troy stands his ground. The man backs his car and leaves. "That fella's up to no good, Buck. If he bothers you again, let me know."

"I forgot my shirt and cap." I hurry back to the dressing room and see Flip has laid my shirt on his bag. "Where's my cap."

"I guess I left it in my bag," Flip says, "Here, I'll get it for you." While flip fumbles in his secret bag, I tell him about the man in the black sedan asking for a player name "Marvin." "Man? What'd he look like?" Flip jerks his head around, his eyes bug out and his head begins to tremor like he's about to have a fit.

"I dunno, I guess like James Cagney in the movies, only taller."

"What'd he say? What'd you say? What'd Troy say? Where'd he go?" Flip screws his neck around getting more and more agitated.

"I don't know, he backed up and left. I can tell he's not from Alabama."

"O my god. Buck, before you go," Flip sheds his spikes, unbuttons his uniform shirt, "I've got some business to attend to and I need you to do something very, very important," his voice reduces to a whisper. He stuffs his uniform into the black bag and zips it shut. Then he buckles his belt around it and tapes the end. "Buck, I need you to take care of this bag for me." His voice changes to a more cultured and refined tone. "Don't let anybody open it until we meet again. I'll return here before the bus leaves, if not, put the bag in my cabinet in the dressing room back home and lock it. The lock and key are inside the cabinet. No matter what happens or who asks about me, don't let anyone touch my bag. Will you do that for me?"

"I guess so."

"No guesswork, Buck. You have to be a man and protect my bag. Are you up to it?"

"Yessir, Flip. I will. . .I mean I am. . .I mean I can."

The players file out so I rush to deliver the bats to the field. Troy Jolly waits for me, "Here, I'll help you tote this bag down the steps. They're kind-a steep."

"What about the flat tire?"

"It's not all the way flat. I'll do it later, but I'm worried about that man who left his manners at home. I promised to see after you. I'd best stick around." He lifts the heavy end of the bag and leads me down the steps. Thunder rolls over heavier than before. "Those dark clouds over yonder don't look promising. Don't think we'll make it through the fifth inning."

The Sylacauga team waits in the field and my team hollers for their bats. We empty the bag on the ground. I leave them scattered and run back to fetch Flip's bag I forgot and left in the locker room. An old man guarding the locked door asks, "He'p you young fella?"

"Coach Flip O'Neal left something for me inside. I come to get it."

He looks me over and asks my name. "Buck, I'm the batboy."

The man rises from his apple crate seat, unlocks the door and reaches inside. "The coach left this for you and told me to make sure you and nobody else gets it."

When I return to the dugout, Digger is hollering for some tape. "Where's Flip, I've gotta tape up my socks. He spies the bag in my hand and reaches for it.

"No, no," I scream and everybody freezes. "There's some in the ball bag." Poco takes me by the arm and pulls me behind the dugout. "What's going on, Buck? Where's Flip?"

The thunder cracks close enough rattle my insides and the wind swirls the trees on the banks outside left field. I tell him about the stranger in the black suit that upset Flip. "Without pointing, look around the grandstand and tell me if you see that stranger." Poco releases my arm and follows me to get a better view.

"I see 'im, standing on the back row close to our dugout," I whisper. Poco walks straight to Jake and Snuffy. One by one they glance over the crowd in the grandstand. Poco sends Jake to home plate to confer with the umpire and the Warriors manager. Then he asks Troy Jolly to follow him up the steps toward the warehouse. A minute later the bus motor cranks and the tires crunch gravel.

Jake and Snuffy settle the Millers down in the dugout and announce they will manage the game until Poco returns with Flip. Jake tacks the lineup card on the wall. "Stretch, you take my place in left field for now. All right, Marty, batter up. Let's play ball."

Marty marches toward home plate and flips the extra bat toward me. Kneeling to rub his hands in the dirt, he presses his ear to the barrel of the crazy bat resting on his shoulder. Instead of standing in the box and taking a few practice swings, this time he remains on one knee when the umpire calls "Play ball." Nothing fazes Marty, not cheering fans and not the umpire calling out "batter up." He refuses to move a muscle. The umpire points to our shortstop and yells, "I said batter up."

After an awkward minute, Marty rises slowly and walks back to the dugout and takes a seat. Snuffy runs over to Marty from the coach's box. "What's wrong with you, man, are you sick?"

"Let Willie hit for me," he says.

I can't do that, you've been announced. The umpire will call Willie out the minute he steps in the box." The veins on Snuffy's neck begin to stand out. The other players urge Marty to go on and step up to the plate, but the stubborn shortstop wraps his arms around the bat and stares into space. Jake Colbert trots from the first base coach's box and catches up with the umpire heading to our dugout. As they approach Marty, a bolt of lightning strikes a tall pine outside the left field fence. Women scream and men curse out loud. The tree crashes across the fence sending a smoke ring into the air. Before I recover my senses, a wall of rain sweeps in from behind the dugout and kicks up dust in its path. Warriors run in from the field and seek refuge in the grandstand instead of their dugout. I scurry to sack the bats and drag them under the dugout shelter.

Steiner warns me not to sack the bats until the game is over, but Speed King says, "This game is over, boys. I've played in this park before. When it rains the water's got no place to go except into this dry lake they call a ball field. We should've headed for the bus at first thunder."

I start to tell Steiner that Troy and Poco took the bus to fix a tire, but Snuffy yells, "Look at the field, it's turning into a dad-gum pond!"

Minutes later, water sloshes over the retainer board of the dirt floor of the dugout. We scramble for standing room on the bench. Ike takes off his spikes, ties them together and hangs them around his neck. That's a good idea, so I do the same.

"Hey you guys, let's make a run for the grandstand," suggests Steiner.

"Too late, we'll get soaked."

"I'm afraid lightning will fry my butt."

"Them Sylacauga boys were smart heading for the grandstand."

"Yeah, look at their dugout, it's full of water."

The chatter goes on above the roar of the rain pounding the dugout roof. Rust colored water streaming down the banks outside the fence fills the basin until the field is completely covered.

The minutes drag on. Water laps at the dugout bench at the feet of grumbling Millers. After an eternity of the heaviest rain

I've ever seen, it drizzles to a stop and a hush falls over the huddled mass in the grandstand. A man calls out, "Are you boys all right?"

"It's Fuzzy Wetzel," exclaims Snuffy, "he never misses a game."

"He's gonna miss this one," quips Steiner.

I peer through the cracks in the dugout's side wall and see Fuzzy with his pants rolled up sloshing through the water. "Mr. Wetzel's coming to the dugout."

"Don't tell me he's walking on water," somebody pipes up laughing.

He faces the team in water almost up to his knees. "Y'all catching anything?" he thrusts his arm forward as if casting a fishing rod. "Well, I reckon not, but I snagged a few suckers up in the grandstand." Fuzzy shows us a wad of paper money in his hat. Passing the hat to reward a Miller's home run is his custom, but this is strange.

"I have been authorized by yon fair and noble baseball fanatics, whom I might add are damp and disappointed at the moment. As I was saying, I'm authorized to offer this handsome prize to any one of you courageous Millers who will demonstrate an extraordinary exhibition of base running skills." A quizzical mumbling breaks loose among the players. "Now hold on, hear me out. To the fortunate volunteer who runs the bases, albeit a bit damp on the field, and slides into home plate goes this prize of an estimated twenty-five dollars." He crushes some bills in his hand as he finishes the challenge.

"He's flipped his wig," mutters Ike Catchings.

"All we wanna do is to evacuate this swamp before the alligators show up, if you don't mind, Mr. Wetzel." Snuffy says.

"How 'bout it Digger, here's your chance to be a star."

"And get rich."

"Yeah, and win a bag of cookies to boot."

The rest of the team eggs Digger on until he gives in. He steps off the bench and examines the hat brimming with money. He slides his spikes from around his neck and tosses them to me. Fully dressed out except for socks and shoes we can't see anyway, Digger sloshes his way out to where home plate should be. The crowd begins to cheer and bellow in unison, "Home run, home run, home run." Fuzzy calls out, "And you have to touch every base and slide into home."

No one would ever know if Digger touches every base as he runs through the flood like a Tennessee walking horse. Instead of sliding into home, he belly flops like my first dive into Hatchet Creek. Recovering his soaked cap from the lake, he lifts it high and flashes his toothy smile at the grateful fans in the grandstand. He wades back to the dugout, points to Snuffy and says, "Tell Maxine to put peanut butter in them cookies."

Chapter 9

Miller players litter the old warehouse benches with wet uniforms and socks waiting for the bus to return. Squeaking brakes outside announce its arrival. Poco bursts through the door and straight to his locker, spikes clicking on the concrete floor. He peels off the soaking wet uniform and slams each piece on a bench. Troy Jolly assures me, "We'll be a little late getting home, but I'll make it right with your folks, Buck." He sits beside me and cracks his knuckles, not a good sign.

The air hangs heavy with wonder, yet no one says a word to Poco about his sudden desertion from the team. No one mentions the long wait for the bus, or being hungry, or Digger's dramatic slide into home. No one gripes about sweeping water off the dressing room floor before changing to dry clothes. The biggest wonder is Flip's absence, but no one dares ask. Poco gets dressed and we file into the Reo like zombies to return to River Bend, a quiet ride except for the tires swishing along the drenched highway.

Poco is first off the bus at the clubhouse. He pushes through the bewildered crowd and disappears into the locker room. Snuffy Veasey announces, "You boys are on your own for supper, we ran too late to stop and eat." The players gripe a bit, but agree to grab some hamburgers at the clubhouse grill upstairs after stowing their gear. Anxious girl friends, wives and people who board players in their homes stretch their necks looking in the bus windows as it empties. Dad steps on board and asks Troy, "Did ol' Blue break down on the road?"

"Naw, the bus made it all right, but I'm not too sure about Poco." I take my time dragging the bat bag and Flip's valise down the aisle so I can hear Troy's story.

"How's that?" Dad asks.

"Something snapped before the game started. He asked me to drive him all over Sylacauga looking for something or somebody. We covered the train depot, the bus terminal, two taxi stands and the police station. The old man said nothing about his intentions the entire trip. He just pointed, grunted and cussed every time he came back empty handed. He was like a crazy man cruising around in a driving rainstorm."

"What about the game?"

"Rained out, but I didn't hear how many innings they got in. Buck, do you know?"

"The rain came before we got started. We all got wetter 'n Monday's washing." I tell about Digger's trot around the bases and his belly flop at home plate, but don't mention the lightning strike. Dad doesn't need an excuse to keep me home next time.

Dad helps me with the bat bag. I stuff Flip's bag into the supply cabinet and snap the lock in the hasp. "Did y'all leave Flip in Sylacauga?" Dad asks Troy who shrugs his shoulders and looks around the locker room.

Ignoring Dad's question, Troy says, "Guess I'd better go tuck ol' Blue back in her garage before she gets arthritis in her ball joints." I figure since Troy said nothing about Poco looking for Flip, I'd better keep my mouth shut. I get busy rubbing down the damp bats with a towel. In Flip's absence I solicit Dad's help collecting the damp and dirty road uniforms scattered about. I go to the equipment cage to get fresh laundry bags and pull the overhead light string. I let out a yelp seeing Poco sitting on Flip's stool.

"Holy moly, Poco, I didn't see you in the dark."

Dad rushes forward. "Poco, are you O. K.?"

The manager slaps his hand over his eyes, blinded by the bright light, but it seems the tears had already done that. He reaches up and pulls the light string. "Too much light, son. What do you need?"

I grab a couple of laundry bags off the shelf and back away. "Nothing, I got 'em."

Dad and I fill the bags and stack them by the door. "See you tomorrow, Poco," I call over my shoulder. No answer. "Do we play Carrollton?" Dad takes one bag to the bin outside and I pick up the other one. As I close the door, a faint, "yep" comes from the equipment cage.

I try to talk Dad into joining the team at the clubhouse grill, but he advises, "You're mother's worried enough as 'tis. Let's don't go flirting with aggravation."

"But I didn't spend my quarter yet."

"Supper's waiting at home, let's go. And, I'll take my quarter back," Dad laughs and probes my pockets. After some horseplay, Dad gets serious. "What got into Poco, Buck?"

"Mr. Wetzel took up a collection and gave the money to Digger to run the bases in the flooded field." I stall to avoid discussing my promise to Flip.

"You already said that, now, what else went on?"

"I didn't tell you about Marty. Even Troy and Poco didn't see that happen."

"Is this about Frog's old bat? What did it do this time?"

"The umpire wanted to start the game early to beat the rain. The wind was blowing hard, but the thunder and clouds weren't too close yet."

"I don't need a weather report, son. What about the bat?"

"I think it told Marty to go to the dugout instead of the batters box."

"What?" Dad stops in the middle of the dark street and grips my arm.

"Yessir, Marty was on deck getting ready to hit when he leaned over and listened to his bat. Then he hustled back to the dugout. No sooner'n he settled on the bench lightning struck a big pine and crashed it on top of the fence."

"How do you know the bat talked, did you hear it or did Marty tell you?"

"Not really. While we waited on the bus to return, Snuffy asked Marty why he refused take his turn at bat. Marty just sits there rubbing that long ol' bat and says, 'I dunno, guess it's my guardian angel looking after me.' All the while he's looking at that crazy bat. I knew what he meant, Dad, I just knew. Then Snuffy tells him he'd better sleep with that angel 'cause Poco will probably suspend him for breaking a rule."

Dad releases his grip on my arm and we continue on our way home. "What was Snuffy doing in charge? Why was he the one to get on Marty's case? Where was. . .? Dad stops as we turn on Laurel Street. A black sedan is parked across from our house at the edge of the streetlight's halo. "Looks like company."

As we draw nearer, I recognize the car. It's the same one that blocked the bus at Sylacauga. Dad peers inside the empty sedan. As he crosses the street toward our house, I lag behind.

"Come on, Buck, your mother's kept supper waiting long enough."

I search for an excuse to avoid facing the mystery man in case he's inside. "I'd better go in the back door because my shoes are caked with mud. I'll leave them on the porch and come on in."

Dad crosses the footbridge and up the steps without answering. I jump the dye ditch and head 'round back. Sensing trouble, I slip off the muddy shoes and tiptoe to the screen door to listen. I hear men's voices but can't make out what's being said until Dad raises his voice.

"If you can't tell me what business you have with my son, then get the blazes out of my house!" I peek through the screen and see the man stands with his back to me. He's the same one Troy tangled with this morning. He utters something I can't make out that sets my Dad off again. "I know the mill owns this house, but I pay rent and have the right to kick your butt out."

The front door slams and I hear tires slinging gravel as the car scratches off. Dad comes to the back porch. "What have you done, son, what have you done?"

"Nothing."

"That fancy dude wanted to ask you some questions, but wouldn't say why. He said he'd be back tomorrow with a Justice of the Peace, so what do you say to that?"

I tell Dad about Troy's tussle with the man earlier. "There has to be something else going on," Dad says.

"He's looking for a man name Marvin, but I don't know anyone by that name."

Mother interrupts, "Y'all come eat supper before it gets cold. I have to get ready for my shift shortly." Dad does not continue drilling me in front of my sisters at the supper table. I retell the story about Digger's idiotic base run, but they find it more gross than amusing.

The mysterious stranger's threat to return with the Justice of the Peace the next morning fades away as the afternoon draws near. Poco calls a meeting with the team before the Carrolton game. Coley, Fuzzy and Carl follow him out of the equipment cage to the locker room where players interrupt dressing out to listen. "Listen up, boys. Snuffy Veasey is the new coach 'til Flip gets back. Now let's go out and play like the winners you can be."

"Hey, Poco, when's Flip coming back. I'm the only hind-catcher left. What's the plan if I get hurt?" Red Mickler asks.

Poco pulls a pouch of Brown's Mule from his back pocket, slices off a plug and stuffs it in his cheek. "Don't get hurt, Red, just don't get hurt."

During the game the Millers put on an exciting exhibition of hitting to start a winning streak of five games, three against Carrolton and a double header against Sylacauga. Scoopy Parker finally learns to avoid excessive balks that give runners extra bases without a pitch. Digger Davis' fastball finds home plate more often than not, only brushing off one batter a game. The wins help the team forget about Flip's absence.

A second double header is set for Saturday, a home stand to make up a rained out game with the Newnan Monarchs. Everyone shows up early, the Millers, the fans and the boys sitting in the trees beyond the left field fence. The Monarchs drag in a little late still smarting from their loss to the Millers the day before. The Friday win over their league leading rivals sends the

Miller's spirits soaring like golden eagles over Lake Martin. Our team's infield delights the fans with a snappy pepper game in front of the grandstand.

During the Miller's infield practice, the Newnan first baseman tries to dull the edge of our player's high spirits with his loud boisterous voice. He stands in front of the visitor dugout rattling off senseless chatter: "Throw the ball to left field! Put on your mama's apron! Rub some glue in your glove!" His ragging has little effect on the Miller infielders except for Marty Davis. He loses his cool and throws the next ground ball at the loudmouth. He sidesteps allowing the ball to scatter the players in the dugout.

"Safe," bellows the opposing first baseman, "safe by a mile."

Poco goes to the Monarchs' dugout to retrieve the errant ball. The Monarchs turn their eyes to sky, ignoring him. "Come on fellas, lemme finish infield, that's a good ball."

"Not any more," someone says and the ball plops out and rests at Poco's feet. The cut-up cover goes in one direction and the naked ball in another. Poco stares at the disemboweled baseball with his mouth hanging open. Then he raises the fungo and charges toward the man who tossed the ball. Red Mickler rushes to grab Poco's belt as the Monarchs bolt to their player's defense. The Millers rally behind Poco and Mickler and several fans charge to the field aching for a fight.

Mickler lowers his facemask and steps between the two managers. "Stop, Stop!" He pushes Poco back and takes command of his fungo bat. "Back off before somebody gets hurt." The players on both teams settle down a bit. Mickler turns to the relieved manager of the Newnan team. "Mr. Manager, I reckon you owe Mr. Walker here a decent ball so he can finish infield practice. The manager looks up and down at Red's built-like-a-bull form before speaking.

"I reckon." He slides his hand into his back pocket and hesitates a moment. The he pulls out a good ball and hands it to Poco. He picks up the remnants of the damaged ball and says, "Fair trade, ol' man, fair trade."

A wry grin spreads across Poco's face. Mickler shouts, "We gotta game to play boys, let's do it. The players lumber back to their respective dugouts.

The truce between the teams lasts only through the first inning. The Millers come to bat in the second with Marty Davis coming to the plate. His hot hitting has earned him fifth in the line-up behind clean-up batter Jake Colbert. Marty's double drives Jake home for the first run of the game. Marty advances to third on the catcher's bad throw and the Monarchs' bench starts to work on his short fuse again. "Steal home, squeeze play!" they call. "Go ahead, you can beat the pitch to the plate!" The ragging takes a negative spin. "He can hit but can't run! You taking root on third base? Did you leave your guts on second base?"

Marty calls time and confers with Poco in the third base coach's box. "Call a squeeze play on the next pitch. I'll teach these Georgia idiots something," he whispers. On the next pitch, Marty takes off for home. The batter misses the signal to bunt and steps aside, the bat never leaves his shoulder. Marty plows into the waiting catcher trying to dislodge the ball. Both players roll in the red dirt and flatten out on their backs. The Monarchs' catcher raises the ball in his hand and Marty is called out. He staggers to his feet and lunges at the catcher. The umpire intervenes and Marty retreats to our bench, picks up his favorite bat and whispers, "Wait 'til next time."

The Monarchs come up to bat in the third inning amid boos from the hometown crowd. Digger casts some verbal darts at the first batter, but Poco stops his chatter. "We don't play that kind of game, son."

"But they're trying to rattle us, we ought-a return the favor." Digger fires back.

"You're playing professional ball now Digger, not high school. You've should've learned by now you can't win a farting contest with a skunk."

Tension mounts between the teams and subsides between innings. With the Millers still leading 1-0, Red Mickler gets set to lead off the bottom of the fifth inning. He hands me his shin guards, chest protector and facemask. After a quick sip of water, he grabs Marty's bat from the dugout and takes a practice swing with two bats in hand. He discards one bat and steps up to the plate. The Monarchs' pitcher says, "Better hang loose in there big man. I don't know where in blazes this pitch is going."

Red backs out of the box and gives his bat the once over. "Did I scare you big man? Get in there and take your chances." The pitcher does not let up.

Red digs his cleats into the batter's box, points his bat at the pitcher and hears a distant voice say, "Throw the ball and duck." On the first pitch, high inside, Red blasts the ball back to the mound hitting the pitcher squarely in the chest. He falls off the mound his body covering the ball and Red's infield hit extends to a double before the third baseman recovers the spent missile.

The manager and coach help the breathless hurler off the field. Red trots over to the dugout for a drink while the relief pitcher tosses warm-ups. I hurriedly pick up the bat and slip it into the dugout before Marty realizes Red got a hit with his guardian angel.

"Good lick, Red, right on the button," Digger applauds.

Red drops the dipper into the bucket. "You don't think I meant to hit him do you?"

"Didn't you point the bat at the pitcher and hit the ball where you aimed, just like Babe Ruth?"

The umpire calls "Play ball." Shaking his head, Red trots out to second to continue the inning. The next three Millers leave Red stranded on base. Trash talking diminishes following the pitcher's misfortune in the fifth. Poco tells Snuffy, "I'll be glad when this game's over. I have a bad feeling in my gut." With only one run in the game, the surly Monarchs are facing another loss, the third in a row, something this powerhouse team is not used to. They score a run in the top of the seventh forcing extra innings if the Millers can't break the tie. Our team leaves three men on base in the seventh without scoring. The first seven-inning game of the double header is forced into an extra inning.

Scoopy Parker retires all three batters with strikeouts in the top of the eight. Bottom of the eighth, two Millers get on base after two outs and Red Mickler walks to the plate with the crowd cheering, "Go Red, Go Red, Go Red!"

"Let's put this one away," Poco yells from the third base coach's box. The pitcher stiffens, slams the ball into his glove and stalks toward third base with his fist drawn like a grenade about to explode.

"What'd you say old man?" snarls the lanky pitcher. "If you want somebody put away, do it yourself if you're man enough." His surprised third base teammate stops the charging pitcher and pushes him back toward the mound. "Come on man, he didn't mean anything personal. It's all chatter, just chatter." The base umpire tells the irate pitcher, "Get back on the mound, son. Play ball."

Red stands in the box. The Monarch's hurler winds up and fires the first pitch behind Red. The Millers jump to their feet and protest the deliberate bean ball. I retrieve the wild pitch and give it to the plate umpire. Red keeps his stance in the batter's box to let the pitcher know his attempted brush off does not intimidate him.

"Atta boy, Red, stand in there and make 'im pitch to you," Snuffy yells. Poco no longer chatters. He bends over and braces his hands on his knees like he doesn't feel too good. Red looks down the third base line for a sign, but Poco does not move. Jake Colbert takes a short lead off second base and shrugs his shoulders, a signal to Poco he doesn't know the next play. But, Poco stares at the pitcher without as much as a twitch. It's as though he's retired from the rest of the game.

The pitcher juggles the rosin bag, tosses it on the ground and steps back on the rubber. Without getting set or checking the runners on first and second, he draws back and fires a fastball straight at Mickler's head. Red, still transfixed on Poco, does not see the ball as it slams against his temple with a sickening thud. He crumples to the dirt without a whimper.

That pitch clears the Millers' bench, some rushing to Red's aid and others go after the smirking pitcher. Monarch infielders hurry to shield their pitcher, but they are outnumbered by charging Millers. The Monarchs in the dugout are slow to react, but soon gather momentum enough to join the melee on the mound, a tangle of arms and legs without form. Bloodthirsty fans hoot and holler as both umpires make futile attempts to unravel the pile of players.

Poco rises from Red Mickler's immobile body and begins to yell to the crowd. The fans calm down enough to hear his plea, "Doctor, doctor, we need a doctor down here!" Troy Jolly rushes to the field carrying a first-aid kit. The mob around the mound back off from their scuffling. Fuzzy Wetzel leaves his box seat and hurries out to view the bean ball victim. After a brief look, he quickly returns and gives his car keys to Coley Farmer. A few minutes later, Coley drives Fuzzy's new station wagon through the utility gate on to home plate. Some men help Poco lift Red's limp body into the back of the station wagon, his face the color of chalk.

With only one out remaining in the inning, the Monarchs' pitcher refuses to return to the mound. His relief walks the next batter and Colbert scores from third on a wild pitch. It's a bittersweet win for our team. During the break between the double-header the managers huddle with the umpires around home plate, probably exchanging lineups for the second game. In a surprise move, Poco walks back to the dugout and tells me to sack the bats and announces, "You boys pack it in, too. The game's called off."

Before anyone can question Poco, Abe Hoffman, the head umpire, stands before the grandstand and holds his mask up for attention. "Due to injuries, the second game is postponed until tomorrow. The first game starts at two o'clock." Although a few muffled groans arise from the fans, their passion for baseball is temporarily suspended by the sight of a favorite player being removed unconscious from the field.

I gather Mickler's facemask, shin guards and chest protector. I start to ask Troy Jolly to help me with the bat bag, but he is busy patching up player's cuts and bruises from the melee. As I bend over to snap on the shin guards, Tad McGee calls my name, "Buck, hey Buck."

He stands by his box seat, his hands clawing into the chicken wire. Shocked at seeing him at the game, I can manage only a weak, "Yeah?"

He shuffles his way over to where I struggle with the hind-catcher's equipment. "I've a mind to help you tote that stuff, if you don't care." Without a word, he slaps the mask on top of his head, slips the chest protector over his head and wedges a shin guard under each arm, just as he had done for his dad years ago. I shoulder the heavy bag of bats and follow Tad past the box where his mother had been watching. "I'm helping Buck 'cause the hind-catcher got hurt," he says. "I'll see you back at the house."

Glistening streams roll down her cheeks as her son takes deliberate steps to re-enter his daddy's world of baseball.

Chapter 10

"Where's your seeing eye dog, Smitty? I don't see him on the bus." The rotund umpire grins without looking behind to see who launched the first shot of teasing he'll bear the remainder of the team's trip to Opelika. Smitty shifts the stub of his cigar from one corner of his mouth to the other and lifts the black leather bag, identical to the one I'm saving for Flip, and shoves it into the luggage rack above the seats. A navy blue umpire's cap slides off his head exposing a shiny dome with a narrow bluish crescent of stubble around back that seems to connect his ears.

"Hey, put this back on your head before you blind me," teases Ike Catchings, returning the umpire's cap.

"And get some tape to hold it in place," adds Squat Steiner.

"You've go no room to talk, Steiner, you're losing so much hair we have to clean the drains after you take a shower."

Steiner rises as if to strike his teammate Ike. Instead, he slaps his hand on his bald spot and says, "Grass never grows on a busy street, does it Smitty?"

Ike laughs, "If I knew what you meant by that remark I'd probably argue."

"You made my point, knucklehead." Steiner has the last word.

Smitty wraps a wide grin around the stub of his cigar. Although he's at the mercy of the players on the bus, payback will come during the game, maybe. While none of the boys doubt Smitty's fairness, the teasing goes on.

"Hey Smitty," Speed King yells from the back of the bus. "I'm pitching today. Before I take the mound, can you tell me the difference between a ball and a strike?"

Smitty reaches in his shirt pocket and takes out a miniature Georgia-Alabama League rulebook. "Let's see now. You wanna know the official definition of balls and strikes. I'm glad to clarify that matter for you Mr. King, even though somebody should've read it to you by now. It says right here on page one of my official rulebook that nothing a pitcher throws is a strike and nothing a pitcher throws is a ball." Smitty rises and aims his pointing finger directly at Speed King. "It ain't a ball, it ain't a strike 'til I call it."

Everyone in the bus breaks out in laughter except Speed who slinks down and pulls his cap over his eyes. The umpire, a revered veteran of the old Textile Mill League, winks at Poco and settles back in his seat to enjoy another conquest over a rookie pitcher.

I am making this road trip against Mother's protest. Citing the dangers that lurk in the shadows of a strange ballpark, she amuses Dad with her exaggerated suspicions. "That Poco, he's the one who let poor Red Mickler almost get killed with a bean ball."

"That pitcher was way outta line. Anyway, nobody's gonna throw baseballs at Buck." Dad winks at me, a signal he's winning the argument. "The other teams are bringing their batboys to Briers Field now that school's out."

Mother rises from her rocking chair and takes a deep breath, letting it out slowly with her eyes closed. "Enough talk, I have to clean up the kitchen. Y'all decide but remember, that guardian angel that watches over baseball fools might miss the bus today."

I sit beside Red Mickler, Flip's usual seat. "It's just a concussion," he says to everyone who asks. "Doc Palmer took a look and sent me home with a tin of aspirin and an ice pack." Poco switches Snuffy back to hind-catcher and asked Red if he feels like coaching first base. "Only 'til the swelling goes down and these spots quit dancing in my eyes," he agrees.

The Trailways bus whirrs across the steel ramp of the river bridge with riveted beams zig-zaging across the side windows. I stand in the aisle to see the river out the back window and notice a black car following the bus. This time we are not in the mill's Reo and Troy Jolly is not here to protect me if the mysterious stranger is the one driving that car.

As we roll into the parking lot between the Opelika Owls' clubhouse and grandstand, I survey the area looking for the black car. I heave a sigh of relief; it's nowhere to be seen. I unload the bats and get ready for the game.

Being the visiting batboy takes some getting used to. Our team dresses out in gray and the Owls wear white uniforms. We enter the field by the home dugout and I almost empty the bat bag in the wrong place. It catches me by surprise that our team goes to the plate first instead of taking the field. I have less time to check equipment and line up the bats before Smitty calls, "Play ball."

During the game I have to remind myself to read the scoreboard upside down since we're not the home team. Although we score more runs than the Owls, I am out of sorts rooting for a winning team dressed in gray uniforms.

Marty slams a homer in the top of the ninth adding another run to our lead. When our side retires we are five runs ahead. The game's in the bag. Speed King has allowed only one run on two hits as he takes the mound in the bottom of the ninth. I can save some time and be ready to board the bus if I put the bats in the bag now.

"I need the bag," I tell Digger, who uses it for a cushion.

"Sure, kid, sure," he says without moving a muscle.

I stand directly in front him to block his view of the action on the field. As he rolls to one side, I jerk the bag from under him and pop it open like a grocery sack.

"Down in front, batboy," a player yells.

I kneel and stretch the bag on the ground alongside the bats. I slide only a couple of bats inside the crumpled bag before a commotion breaks out in right field. Jimmy Glover calls time and waves his hand frantically, shouting as he darts across the infield and pitcher's mound. At first, I think he's protesting a call by the umpire. Smitty jerks off his mask and looks at me. Suddenly, the whole team starts screaming at me.

I look around trying to make sense of the fuss. Glover rushes up and snatches the bag from my hand. With one swift jerk, he empties the bats on the ground and slings the sack in my face.

"It's bad luck to sack the bats before the game's over, boy," he screams. I sink to my knees trying to drown out the mutterings of disgust from the players as they take their places and resume the game. It is clear this is not another playful initiation, no one is laughing.

I remain on my knees until Speed fans the last Owl, ending the longest half inning of my career as batboy. Everyone leaves the dugout to get dressed except Snuffy Veazey. I feel his hand on my shoulder not knowing if the abuse will continue or I'm in store for a pity party.

"Come on Buck, let's secure the bats and head for home." He holds the bag open as I drop the bats in one by one. "Don't worry, 'twas an honest mistake, anybody could make it. Baseball players are a superstitious bunch. Sometimes I think they need a witch doctor instead of a manager." Snuffy's soft words almost bring tears to my eyes. I manage to fight off crying, but it's hard to get over being treated like a dog with the mange in front of a thousand people. "I should've told you that it's bad luck to sack the bats before the last out. My fault."

Rose Hill Steak House is only ten minutes from the ballpark, but the ride is ten minutes too long for me. Nobody speaks to me as I slink down and try to become part of the upholstery. The hungry team wastes no time emptying the bus at the café, but I remain behind to suffer in silence. Snuffy comes back to the bus. "Time to put on the feed bag, Buck."

"I'm not hungry."

"Too late, I ordered you a steak."

The waitress in the green dress comes to the table and stuffs a lock of rusty hair back under the hairnet. "How do y'all want ya steaks cooked, I forgot to ask?"

"Just cut the horns off a steer and lead 'im to the table," Digger sounds off. The unimpressed lady counts three rare, four medium and three well-done and moves to the other table.

"How many want rare?" she asks.

"It don't matter, honey, John's gonna burn every one anyway," Jimmy Glover shouts for everyone to hear. My chest tightens as I'm about to witness this right fielder embarrass another defenseless person like he did to me on the field today. I wish I had stayed in the bus.

The swinging doors to the kitchen suddenly fly open and a short stocky man rushes toward Jimmy waving a meat cleaver over his head and shoutin, "Thassa las' time you gonna make fun 'a big John." With a quick swipe of his left hand, he gathers a handful of Jimmy's bushy hair from behind. "I'm-a gonna make-a me a new dust mop."

Jimmy's getting what's coming to him now, but scalping seems too drastic, even for a smart aleck. He leans back in his chair, not scared, but laughing. "Calf's rope, John, calf's rope," he cries.

"You gave up just in time Jimbo," the cook laughs. He releases his grip and heads back to the kitchen.

"Last year, I worked for John. He tried to make a cook outta me but I chose baseball instead," Jimmy explains.

Digger walks over to Jimmy, pats him on the shoulder and slips something into his water glass. "Bad decision ol' buddy, you should've listened to him." Then he steps back pointing to Jimmy's glass of water. "Look everybody, Jimmy's caught a fly, first one all day." A fake ice cube with a housefly inside floats in Jimmy's water.

The waitress begins serving T-bone steaks that almost cover the platters. She sets the largest one before Speed. "The winning pitcher gets the most beef," she says.

"That lady's got an eye for baby pitchers," Squat teases.

"Watch your mouth, Steiner, that's John's wife. He won't think twice about circumcising you with that meat cleaver," warns Jimmy.

"Too late for that," Steiner chuckles.

Real steaks like this are never cooked at my house, only meat loaf, hamburger and round steak Mother beats tender with the edge of a saucer. I watch the others and cut small pieces to force down my throat already choked with misery.

"You done with this, son?" the waitress removes my platter and replaces it with a green slip of paper. I slip it off the table wondering if I have to pay for my own meal. The check is not for my meal, it's for twenty. Now, I'm really in trouble. Is this my punishment for goofing up in the game?

"Thanks for the steak, Buck, it was delicious," bellows Digger. The rest of the players at my table except Poco push their chairs back thanking me as they make haste out the door.

"I hope you brought your money belt," someone adds from behind my back.

"I look up at the waitress standing with her arms crossed and a stern look on her face. "I only got fifty cents, m'am," I fumble in my pocket.

"I figure a month washing dishes will take care of the bill, son," she says.

I feel a hand nudging my knee. Poco slips a wad of bills under the table into my lap and whispers, "Don't forget to tip the lady."

She begins to laugh and help me sort the money for the bill. "I really didn't wanna do that to you, honey, but it really was funny to see the look on your face."

Poco takes the money pouch over to the next table to settle up with the Trailways driver.

"Where'd you hide my brother, Poco?" snarls the man in the black suit who had slipped unnoticed inside the café.

Poco looks up and quickly shoves the team's share of the gate receipts back inside the pouch and zips it shut. Then he jumps to his feet and says, "Everybody on the bus, right now."

The stranger grabs Poco by the arm forcing him to drop the money pouch and the man places his shoe on it. "Answer my question, baseball man." As Poco lunges to retrieve the money, the man parries his thrust sending Poco across a table and onto the floor.

"The bus driver takes my arm and says, "Let's get outta here, lad before somebody gets hurt."

"Stay where you are, boy," the man yells, "you know something about Marvin."

I resist the urge to abandon Poco, to leave him at the mercy of this mad man from hades. He picks up the money pouch and comes toward me. "Hold it right there, mister, you ain't going nowhere with that money bag." John comes through the swinging doors waving his meat cleaver like before, only this time he's dead serious.

The man pitches the pouch at Poco who's back on his feet. "No, no, you got it all wrong. I don't want the money, I just want to know where these two are hiding my wife's brother."

John stands firm, "Looks like a robbery to me. Now you just set down and wait for the police, they're on the way."

The man darts out the entrance. When John starts after him, Poco say, "Let 'im go John. He's not after money. This is a personal matter between him and me. I'll handle it."

"What about the boy?" the cook's wife expresses concern for my safety.

The bus driver leads some players back inside armed with baseball bats. "Where's the robber?" one asks.

John says, "O yeah, a lotta help you boys are. Robin Hood ran right past y'all and got away."

Poco takes a seat beside me on the bus. "You 'n me have to talk when we get back to the clubhouse." Coley Farmer waits outside the River Bend dressing room as the bus pulls up. Snuffy offers to help me with the bats and other equipment, but Poco hands him the money pouch, "Take this to Coley. I'll help Buck."

I drag the bat bag to the front of the bus. Poco says, "Seems to me you've got something that fella in the black suit wants. What is it?"

"I dunno."

He rubs the stubble on his chin and shakes his head. "Now, Buck, you're not as dumb as you try to look. This has to do with Flip's sudden disappearance at Sylacauga, doesn't it?"

"Reckon it might, but it might not. But that's where I first saw that man who pushed you down at Rose Hill. When I told Flip about him, he got real nervous and skipped the game."

"Did he give you any clue about where he was going?"

"No sir. He just said he had some business to take care of and he'd come back later for his. . .I mean. . ."

"For his what?"

"Sorry, I'm not supposed to tell anybody that secret, even my Dad. And he's not happy about that at all."

"You're talking about Flip's black bag you locked up in the cage, aren't you?" I try to turn my face to stone so he can't read yes or no in it. "I know what Flip has in his bag. He keeps no secrets from me. If you know where he went tell me so I can find him before that stranger does."

"He didn't tell me, honest. Is Flip in some kind of trouble? Did he. . ."

"No nothing like that."

"Then why's that man looking for him?"

The bus driver returns to the bus. "We're getting out," Poco says, gripping the strap on the bat bag and leading the way to the dressing room. As we stow the gear, Poco adds, "If you hear from Flip, I want to be the first one to know and I want your promise on that."

"Scout's honor, Poco."

Chapter 11

Field Day is Fuzzy's idea, a fun way to revive River Bend's lagging baseball spirit and to boost attendance at home games. "It works like this," he spits out words around his freshly lit cigar. "We fill Briers Field with people, some who've never seen a game, and the team will get so fired up they'll win the game and many more." He removes the cigar to dream a little bigger. "It looks like we have a chance to host the All-Star Game and rake in a ton of money."

"We have to lead the league by July third to play in the All-Star game. Don't forget we've got four games against Griffin coming up. They took the lead from Newnan last week and shoved us back to third place." Poco tries to calm Fuzzy down with a reality check, but the pumped up big mule ignores him.

"Look, Poco, I've done the figures. If we sweep Carrolton this week and if Griffin loses three games, we're in the money. I know the odds are against us, but we can pull it off, can't we fellas?"

My head swims in the flood of all those wins and losses and the other two Big Mules scratch their heads as Fuzzy rattles on. Finally, Coley Farmer cottons to the idea of a field day and suggests, "We'll get the Chamber of Commerce gang to buy a stack of tickets and give them to their customers.

Carl Craig chimes in, "I'll print up some arm bands for the merchants to wear on game days that read 'Baseball Tonight'." He looks my way as I stuff clean towels in the lockers getting ready for tomorrow's game. "What do you think of our plan for a field day, Buck?" I grin and nod, not admitting being lost in the whole discussion a while back.

Poco waits until after the game to pop the news about the upcoming field day. "Before we play ball there'll be contests between the two teams and all kinds of entertainment for the crowd," he says to the team before they head to the showers, all excited about their shutout against Carrollton.

"I can get my brother's hillbilly band to play between innings. He'll do it for free," Scoopy Parker drawls dropping his size thirteen spikes on the dressing room floor.

"And bring on some cheerleaders with short skirts," adds Digger Davis as he wraps a towel around his head and sways his naked frame back and forth.

"Now that will draw a real baseball crowd," scoffs Snuffy.

"All right, enough. We won't need outsiders to distract fans that pay to see a ball game," Poco stops the foolishness. "We've got talent right here in this room we can show off competing against LaGrange."

"You mean like the Olympics, Poco?"

"No, you got it wrong, Ike. It'll be like Digger sliding into home under a foot of water," Squat Steiner howls, looking around to see who's laughing with him.

"That's it, boys. Get showered and dressed."

Coley Farmer hands Poco a slip of paper after the last player leaves the room. "Hmm, not bad for a weekday," Poco says, "'bout the same as yesterday." They discuss the game receipts and then Coley offers to help Poco plan the upcoming field day. "Thanks, but I'll handle it. If I need help I'll call you."

Coley changes the subject. "Oh, by the way, I had a call from the owner of a Class B team in Virginia. Marty Davis is considering an offer to move up a notch."

"Damn, he's our best hitter. Can he just pick up and move without notice?"

"According to league rules he can. You remember we don't have contracts like the big leagues. Can you find a replacement in the middle of the season?"

"I'll see if Marty'll wait 'til after the All-star game. We've got plenty of infielders, but we need an extra player behind the plate, one that can hit. I don't think Mickler's dizzy spells are going away anytime soon." I wonder if Marty plans to take the crazy bat along with him, since nobody else hits with it.

Excitement builds up two days before Saturday's field day competition thanks to the *River Bend Lookout* edition that hit the streets mid-day on Thursday. The front-page story announces the first night game will be played at Briers Field on Friday. All week I had watched River Bend Electric Company install the single crossbars of shaded light bulbs on creosote poles that encircle the field from one end of the grandstand to the other. In addition, Friday night will be Ladies' Night, with free admission for every woman escorted by a gentleman that buys a ticket. The most exciting team news is embedded deeper in the story: *The Millers are now in second place in the league and winning the next two games will put us within sight of first place.*

The dressing room turns into a madhouse following our win on Friday night. "We've gotta win tomorrow," Digger revels, "First place, I can taste it." Poco urges the players to get dressed and take their celebration upstairs to the clubhouse grill. I get busy gathering towels and brushing dirt off the white uniforms. There's no time to launder them before Saturday's game.

"Buck, I'll need you to show up early tomorrow and help set the stations for the field day contests. Go by a grocery store on your way and find a couple more empty bushel baskets." Poco retreats to the cage to map out plans for the competitions.

On game day I find empty bushel baskets at A&P and bring them to the clubhouse. A new Ford sedan with a U. S. government license plate is parked behind Poco's car. I find two men in suits poking around the dressing room as I struggle to wedge the baskets through the door.

"Good morning, boy," the taller one says reaching out to hold the door open for me. "Are you making a delivery?"

I look around for Poco, but he's not here. "I'm the batboy."

"We need to talk with Mr. Walker. When do you expect him in?" The taller man does the talking while the other one cases the shower room.

"His car's outside."

"Yes, I know, but he's not. . ."

The man still holds the door open as Poco appears behind him. "Can I help you?" Poco asks. The man wheels around and shoves one hand inside his coat, then slowly withdraws it and offers Poco a handshake.

"You'd be Mr. Walker?" he shakes Poco's hand. "I'm agent Sisson and that's my partner, agent Warren. We're from the Federal Bureau of Investigation." Both men flash their badges.

Poco crosses over to his locker. "You gentlemen catch me at a bad time. I have a game coming up shortly and. . ."

“This won’t take long,” Sisson reaches for a manila envelope in Warren’s hand and extracts a photograph. “Have you seen this man?”

Without looking at the picture, Poco proceeds to undress. “I know you boys have a job to do, but so do I. Why don’t we discuss your business after the game? I’ll still be here.” He reaches into his locker and withdraws two tickets. “Here’s a couple of passes. Enjoy the game and I’ll meet you right here afterwards.”

Warren bristles and grabs Poco’s shirt collar, “You know, Walker, we can hold you right here all day if necessary.” Sisson signals Warren to release Poco and takes the tickets.

“I think it’s time we take in a baseball game. Don’t plan on leaving town Mr. Walker.” They walk out eyeing their free passes.

Poco puts on his game uniform and picks up his treasured bag of baseballs. “You grab the bats, Buck, and I’ll carry these baskets to the park. This day’s gonna be a doozy.”

As we set up the field for the contests, early arriving fans begin to fill the grandstand and bleachers. Boys my age carry heavy bins of ice covered bottles of Nesbitt Orange, Nehi Grapes and Co-colas strapped across their shoulders. Others hawk nickel sacks of parched peanuts from newspaper carrier bags. I empty the bat bag and begin lining up the bats when Tad McGee rushes to my side out of breath. “Buck somebody’s startin’ a fight over yonder.” He points to the corner of the grandstand nearest the visiting team’s dugout. A group of men crowd around front row seats raising their arms and shouting. Tad and I run closer to investigate.

“His kind belongs out there in the bleachers,” the leader of the protest yells. I cannot see the object of his angry jabs, so I press closer against the chicken wire barrier. A tall player in a gray uniform pushes his way through the boisterous crowd and stands on the second row of seats. He waves the people back with a baseball bat.

"You people settle down and listen to me," he shouts in a clipped accent. "This man's going to sit right here and watch our team play, or there won't be any ball game." The protesters moan and grumble.

One man says, "And who are you to give orders?"

Fuzzy Wetzel speaks up, "I can tell you're not from these parts young fella. You oughta know colored folk sit in the bleachers."

"Sir, if Sergeant Washburn here is good enough to fight for our country, then he's good enough to sit in the grandstand." The grousing dies down as the men begin to shrug their shoulders and shuffle their feet. Some return to their seats which thins out the crowd enough for me to see two heavily decorated army paratroopers, one is black, sitting on the first row. A couple more LaGrange players armed with bats gather around to support their teammate's threat to cancel the game, if necessary.

Fuzzy resigns his futile protest, "All right folks, there's nothing in the rulebook that says our Indian friend here can't sit in the shade and watch the ballgame."

Tad whispers, "But that soldier's not an Indian, he's a. . ."

Squat Steiner interrupts standing behind us, "Never mind boys, Fuzzy's just made it possible for you guys to witness history being made right here in River Bend." He chuckles and tugs us by the collars, a sign to get back to business.

"Welcome to Briers Field, home of the River Bend Millers." Bull Ingram's voice booms from the two huge speakers suspended from the grandstand rafters. "On behalf of the Chamber of Commerce and WRSF, we are privileged to witness the first annual field day, contests that will demonstrate before your eyes the basic skills of the art and craft of America's favorite pastime, baseball."

Tad helps me set up the finish line ribbon for the pitchers' race. Poco schedules ten events pitting select players from each team. Jake Colbert beats his LaGrange centerfielder by throwing six out of ten balls into baskets behind home plate from deep center field. The LaGrange hind-catcher rings the nail keg behind second base four out of ten throws defeating Red Mickler who still suffers spells caused by the bean ball.

Digger Davis wins the pitchers' sprint hands down. Ted Rich stumbles on second base losing the base run by two seconds. Marty Davis' funny bat captures the longest ball derby with two of five hits over the right field fence. The games wind down to two remaining events—the managers' fungo duel and hot pepper. Poco and his younger opponent take turns trying to hit fly balls into lime circles drawn in center field. Poco places the first one on the money, but misses the next nine. The LaGrange manager's flies don't even come close to the target.

"And now the final event of these thrilling exhibitions of baseball skills," Bull announces. "It's one reserved for you fans. Let's hear a cheer for h-o-t-p-e-p-p-e-r, hot pepper. We need ten volunteers, five Miller fans and five Cracker fans." Half-dozen men wander out to home plate greeted by Snuffy Veasy and the LaGrange coach. "Where are you old-timers who played baseball? Step forward and show the fans you've still got plenty of steam left in the boiler." Three more men including the black soldier stride onto the field. A loud gasp rising from the grandstand is offset by cheers from the bleachers. It takes a minute for Bull Ingram to regain his composure. With a signal from Snuffy, Bull announces, "We need one more competitor from the Miller side of the grandstand." No one stirs. "One more sure-handed soul, folks. We can't let our team down. The games are all tied. The winner of the hot pepper game will show who's...wait a minute, what's this?"

Peggy Sue Slater darts from the grandstand clutching her daddy's first base pad with one hand and holding her dress down with the other. "Well, I'll be darn," Bull gasps into the microphone. "What do we have here?" Peggy Sue stands in the vacant slot facing Snuffy Veasey popping her fist in the pad. "Miss, miss, I'm not sure you want to. . .I mean with all those men. . ." One fan begins rapping his bottle against the grandstand seat. Soon a thunder of bottles hitting wood drowns out Bull's objections. "O.K., O.K., Bull relents, let's get on with the show. Here're the rules of the game. The two coaches will take turns batting ground balls to their teams. Now, y'all need to spread out some more. Each player has to field the ball closest to him, or...uh her, as the case may be and toss it back to the opposing team's coach. Any player that misses the ball will be tagged with an error. Two errors and you're out of the game. The last man, or girl," Bull muffles a giggle with a cough, "standing will be the winner for his team."

"Or her team," a woman shouts from the grandstand.

"Oh, yeah, yeah. All right, Coach Veasey give each competitor a glove and let's get. . .I mean, play ball!" Snuffy circles the air with his hand looking at the press box. "Oh, I need to remind y'all, the game gets faster as it goes along. That's why it's called hot pepper."

The coaches take turns hitting easy grounders to their teams, but Snuffy skips Peggy Sue each round. She keeps on popping her glove on ready, but no balls come her way. Two men from each team are called out and some young women in the grandstand begin chanting, "Hit it to the girl; hit it to the girl." Soon some men join the chant. Another from the Millers side is eliminated leaving one man and Peggy Sue to defend against three LaGrange fans.

"Come on, Mr. Veasey, I've got a glove," Peggy Sue protests after Snuffy finally hits a ball in her direction, a slow roller anyone could field. "Burn me one."

The cheers grow louder as the grounders zip by every contestant except one on each team—Peggy Sue and the soldier. The LaGrange coach steps up out of turn and yells, "Look out, young lady, here comes a hot one." He slams a rocket shot at her aiming to force her first error, but she snags it and flings the ball back to him so hard that he swings and misses. The crowd roars as the ball ricochets off the grandstand wall and hits him in the back.

Fuzzy Wetzel has seen enough. The pepper match comes down to a black man and a teenage girl, more than he can stand. He signals to Bull Ingram to stop the game. "What say folks, let's call it a draw."

"No, no," the fans object. "Let 'em go." Fuzzy shrugs his shoulder and gives up. The army sergeant misses his second hot grounder and turns to congratulate Peggy Sue. She backs away, but then extends her hand, glove and all, to shake hands. The crowd roars their approval.

Fuzzy hands Peggy Sue a blue ribbon and the soldier a red one. As he turns to walk back to his box seat someone from the

LaGrange dugout hollers, "Ain't ya' gonna shake their hands, mister?"

Bull Ingram intervenes with his own announcement. "Ladies and Gentlemen, I have just been informed that the winner of the hot pepper contest is Peggy Sue Slater, daughter of that great Chief's first baseman, Hook Slater, may he rest in peace. Let's give her a big hand folks."

Peggy Sue's moment of fame lasts only as long as it takes her to return to her seat in the grandstand. Her mother rips the blue ribbon from her hand and shakes a finger in her face. River Bend's newest baseball star throws her daddy's glove at her mother's feet and leaps up the steps and out of Briers Field. If she is gone for good, I've lost my best foul ball retriever for the rest of the game.

We beat LaGrange by three runs before an appreciative field day crowd, but the team's celebration is guarded as they await the results of another game at Opelika. Poco asks Dad to delay his call to the newspaper until the results of the Opelika-Griffin game are posted. "If Griffin loses we get to host the All-Star Game. You can call me at Carl's house later," Poco says.

My elation over the win made me forget about Poco's meeting with the F.B.I. agents. As we arrive at the clubhouse, the government car is still parked in the road and Coley Farmer is passing out Tampa Nugget cigars, congratulating the players.

"And here's our illustrious manager, boys, Mr. Poco Walker. Here, have a cigar." Coley offers the box to Poco.

"Let's hold off until we hear if Griffin lost. They may be. . ."

Coley interrupts, "Don't worry, I just called the press box at Opelika and Griffin's behind by three runs in the top of the ninth."

A cheer rattles the dressing room. "And the bottom of the batting order is up for the Pimentos."

I think of the Owls' batboy and hope he won't sack the bats before the last out and jinx his team. I catch myself becoming infected with baseball's superstitions that I've learned to hate.

"Coley, you know the game ain't over yet," Snuffy warns.

"Yeah, but you and the boys ought-a get your spikes shined up and your jockey straps washed before next Wednesday."

Poco stands on a bench. "Turn off the showers and huddle up for a minute. This won't take long." In a rare display of appreciation, Poco removes his cap and says, "You boys have done me proud. You've come a long way and here're the facts. If Griffin loses tonight, you'll have two days off and we'll practice Tuesday just to smooth out the rough edges. If Griffin wins, *y'all,* hey, listen to me sounding like Johnny Reb." Everyone laughs and Digger lets loose a Rebel yell. "Anyway, if we don't host the All-Star game every one of you will have five days off except for our own all-stars, Marty and Digger."

"Almost makes me wish Griffin would win," laughs Snuffy. He ducks away from his teammate tossing towels at his head.

"The second half of the season starts Saturday, so we'll practice Friday. Just one more thing, boys, Flip would've been as proud as I am." Poco steps off the bench and covers his sweaty head with a towel.

I collect damp towels and uniforms smudged with red dirt while Coley Farmer tries to talk with Poco about plans for the All-Star game. "Coley, I've got a little business to take care of right now, so let's meet at Carl's house later." Poco ushers him to the door.

After stacking the bulging laundry bags by the door, I ask Poco if he needs anything else. "Buck, can you find another empty laundry bag back there?" he gestures toward the cage.

"I'll look." Poco joins me in the equipment cage and takes the key to Flip's locker where I hid it. I offer him the empty bag as he removes the lock.

"Buck, I want you to take a bag of laundry home with you tonight." His strange request makes the cat get my tongue. "Open it up," he says. I pop open the bag. He removes Flip's black satchel and drops it into the bag. "Here's your laundry," he says, drawing the strings tight and doubling the knot.

"Yessir, but. . ."

"I know how strange this seems, son, but I need you to follow my exact instructions quickly and without question. I'll explain later."

"Betcha britches."

The dressing room door creaks. "Come on in, gentlemen," Poco greets the g-men. "I'll be finished here in a jiffy." He picks up a full laundry bag by the door and motions me to bring along the one in my hand. With Flip's satchel concealed inside, I take the bag, walk by the two agents and wonder if Poco has tricked me into breaking the law.

Poco unlocks the trunk of his car and tosses the dirty laundry inside. "Now, set your bag on the ground and bring me the other two," he says in a hushed tone. "Listen closely, I'm going in to talk with those men. You put the dirty laundry in my car, close the trunk and turn the handle. Take that bag I gave you home with you. Do you understand?"

"Yessir, but, but. . ."

"Stop sounding like a motor boat. Do like I tell you and whatever you do, say nothing about this to anyone."

The agents watch me closely as I retrieve the remaining laundry bags, but Poco whisks me out of the dressing room quickly. "Run on home and tell your mama I didn't mean to keep you so late. See you next week."

When I get home Dad is too busy on the telephone to notice my bag of "laundry," but Annie asks, "What 'cha got in the sack, Buck, some more crazy bats?"

Mother orders me out of the house to my delight. "Take that baseball junk out to the porch and leave it. There's no more room in the house."

I go out the back door and hide the bag in my secret den under the house. Dad seems to be arguing with someone on the phone when I return. "Yeah, I know, but that game doesn't matter. Fuzzy got it all wrong." Finally, he hangs up and joins us at the supper table.

"What did Mr. Wetzel get wrong, Dad?"

Before Dad can answer, Bobbie Jean exclaims, "Did y'all see Peggy Sue beat those men playing that game today?"

"That is quite enough baseball talk at the table, especially about a shameless girl showing her fanny in front of all those folks."

"Aw, Mother, she was something. . ."

"Now Bobbie Jean, don't you go getting any notion about playing baseball or any other ball. There're enough crazy folks in this house as 'tis," Mother puts a damper on Dad and me reliving today's game with all its twists and turns. I am not disappointed because I need some time to think of a story to tell Dad about the laundry bag under the house, a version that skips around the truth without telling a lie.

Chapter 12

The All-Star game at Griffin, Georgia turns out to be a none-event for folks in River Bend. Fuzzy Wetzel had gotten everyone's hopes up with miscalculations. Although the Millers had won one more game than the Pimentos, we had lost one more than they had. Dad explained that the League calculates team standings by percentages and the Millers missed hosting the All-Star game by a hair. It doesn't seem fair to me but I'm more concerned with returning the laundry bag to Poco before worry burns a hole in my brain.

Friday morning I snake through the village like a bandit and hide the laundry bag behind a shed next to the dressing room. After checking to be sure the g-men's car is gone, I retrieve the bag and bring it inside. "You're here early, Buck, good." Poco separates game balls from practice balls in the equipment cage. "Just park the bag anywhere in here."

His lack of caution surprises me. He doesn't whisper or check to see if I've been followed. He says nothing about the mysterious black bag that I took great chances to hide. He doesn't even say thank you. He's too occupied with his precious baseballs to answer the questions eating holes in my gut. I decide to straighten out the benches and distribute fresh towels before the team arrives to dress out.

Marty fails to show up for practice along with Lane, Glover and Lakestraw. "Those boys went to the beach," Snuffy explains, "but I don't know what happened to Marty."

"The beach?" Poco exclaims, "What in the devil got into them?"

"They went on the company bus to the mill camp at Panama City and it's not due back 'til tonight."

"I'll be damned. I'd suspend their butts if I didn't need them for the game."

Practice is about as ho-hum as a history lecture. Back in the dressing room, my plan to ask Poco about Flip's black bag is stymied by an argument with Coley Farmer. They are still at it when I finish stacking the dirty laundry in the bin so I mosey on home.

Saturday morning I find out what the argument was about. Coley gathers the team around him in the clubhouse and apologizes for his mistake. "I'm really sorry, boys, but I didn't order a bus for this trip. I misread the schedule and thought we would play at home today and tomorrow."

"So we hafta walk to Lanett, huh?" asks Digger.

"No, no, Fuzzy's out rounding up cars, so just hang loose 'til he gets back."

"I want a Cadillac."

"I'll take a Buick."

"And a pick-up truck for me."

A car pulls up in front and the players scramble to claim choice seats. Soon a string of cars line the road. Fuzzy arranged for Dad and Troy Jolly to drive used Studebakers from his car lot. Despite the makeshift travel arrangements everyone is in a good mood, especially since the team is anxious to clobber the last place Lanett Weavers.

We win both games at Lanett traveling both days in cars to save money. Poco calls a team meeting for Monday afternoon.

"We'll meet in the high school cafeteria for an early supper thanks to the generosity of Paul Alexander and Mayfair Mill."

Dad takes me along to return Fuzzy's car to the lot and we walk across the street to the high school. Although we have no reason to attend the team meeting, Poco says we are welcome to come. "You might enjoy the little surprise we have for the team."

Poco and Snuffy are huddled with the big mules around a table as we enter the cafeteria. Hearing the door open, they quickly slam lids on gray boxes lined along the table.

"Good, we've got some help." Fuzzy waves Dad and me over and begins shoving chairs toward us as Paul Alexander stacks the boxes on the floor. "Y'all arrange these chairs around those two long tables, figure thirty should be plenty."

We finish our set up and players begin to file in. Fuzzy directs each one to a yellow Nehi box where he had iced down bottles of R. C.'s and orange sodas. Settling at the tables we turn to face Poco who raps a bottle on the table. He addresses the assembly with a sly grin and a twinkle in his eye. "Listen up y'all," a burst of laughter follows his use of the southern greeting. "I'm sure everybody knows these gentlemen standing here beside me, Mr. Farmer, Mr. Wetzel, Mr. Alexander and Mr. Craig, they run the business end of our club. I called this meeting at their request. Who's going first, Mr. Coley?"

Coley Farmer advises the players they should be aware of the club's financial condition, so he drones on reading the current report of receipts and expenses. Carl Craig shares a summary of team statistics. Fuzzy tries to liven up the meeting with an off-color story. "Seems that Ty Cobb met the rookie Harry-the-hat Walker and ribbed him about being from Alabama. He said, 'Walker, do you know what we do to boys named Harry over in

Georgia?' Harry says, 'Naw, but I know what we do with Cobbs in Alabama.'"

Poco pats Fuzzy on the back without cracking a smile. "Just what we need, a little Southern humor that we out-of-state boys don't understand." The players respond with muted applause. "We need to move on to the business at hand. First, I am not pleased to report that Marty Davis will probably not finish out the season with us. He's up in Richmond trying out for 'B' ball." Oo's and ah's ripple throughout the cafeteria. I wonder if he took the mysterious bat with him. "But he may come back if things don't work out."

Poco pulls a gray box from under the table. "Before we're served the delicious steak dinner Mayfair Mill is providing, I'm proud to present the Mill's President Mr. Paul Alexander." He hands the box to Paul and steps aside still wearing that quirky grin.

"Fellow baseball fans," a brief pause for chuckles, "You've heard the figures from Coley. The club is operating at a break-even point, just barely paying its bills. The solution to our problem is simple, we have to do something to make sure people continue to come watch y'all play ball."

"Are we gonna have another field day, Mr. Alexander?" asks Steiner.

"Yeah, I wanna see that filly play hot pepper again," Digger adds clapping his hands over his head.

"No, boys, nothing like that. We've come up with a better plan. As you know, Mayfair Mill is a leader in making knit goods for ordinary consumers as well as a few sports teams."

"He means underwear," Digger snickers. "I know 'cause I work there."

Paul ignores his remark. "We are preparing to launch a campaign to produce a line of uniforms that will capture the United States sporting goods market. Our artist has developed a new style for baseball uniforms and we want the Millers to model this innovative design first, give them a test drive, so to speak."

"Fresh new uniforms, that sounds great!" Snuffy cheers.

Paul removes the top of the square gray box. "Here, feast your eyes on this," he says lifting a white shirt trimmed with bold red piping and holds it by the shoulders. The letters, RBM, are bunched together in Old English style like my Dad's Masonic Bible. The numerals on back are just as fancy.

"What's different besides the elaborate letters and numbers?" Ike Catchings asks.

Paul lifts the shirt higher. "Notice, no shirttails, no need to tuck it in your pants. This elastic band keeps it snug around your waist. Just wait 'til you see the pants. Poco, hand me that other box. Here we go."

"Short pants!" the players utter in unison.

"Hold on boys," Poco yells, "Before we can hit the field in these new uniforms Sunday, we need to check with Commissioner Decatur and Opelika's manager. I don't want us to forfeit the game for being out of uniform."

The big mules score a hit. The gimmick causes a run on tickets, at least for one game. The League Commissioner brings a delegation from Chattahoochee Valley to witness the spectacle. There is a surge in female fans, some dragging their husbands along. River Bend is not known for stylish men's wear, so there's talk of the Millers starting a new fashion trend in men's clothing. But around here men don't dress up for baseball games, they show up in their work or fishing outfits.

The team chooses Digger Davis to lead them onto the field for their initial appearance before a grandstand surging with fans. His introduction is met with wolf whistles, cat calls and laughter. Digger crosses home plate before realizing he is alone. He comes to a halt, turns as red as the warm-up jacket across his shoulder and tries to wave his comrades to join him. They finally trot out with heads down, cursing the mixed reception. The Opelika players add to their misery with sneers and jeers. "I thought we came to play men, not little boys. Your slip is showing. I've seen better legs on kitchen tables."

The grand fashion show is the least of the Millers' problems today. Ted Rich gets on base first with a single. He skins his left thigh stealing second and leaves bloodstains on his new short pants. Ike's sliding pads droop below his pants like long underwear. Jackie House and Bo Turner spend the top of the first inning tugging at their sagging long socks. "Ain't no way to keep these socks up without real baseball knickers," Jackie complains.

"Especially when you ain't got no muscles in your legs," Steiner chuckles.

I try to solve their problem with strips of tape that come loose when they run. Other problems arise as the game goes on. Dropping to one knee in the on-deck circle is painful, so waiting batters have to either stand or squat like a hind-catcher.

Poco has enough of these distractions. He huddles the players in the dugout before they come to bat in the bottom of the third inning. "You guys are handling the ball but you're not making the plays. You've got to get your heads in the game. Quit making mental mistakes. Get the bat off your shoulder and swing at good pitches instead of watching them go by. Just because your knobby knees are showing doesn't mean you're running around naked. Now go and get some hits, act like ball players instead of a bunch of clowns. Play hard ball for a change and shake them Owls off their perches."

The Millers jack up their game with more aggressive playing and win by two runs. But the dressing room becomes like a combat zone. Snuffy and Red Mickler treat skinned legs with mercurochrome accompanied by yelps of pain from their victims. Dad and I help some apply liniment to charley-horses caused by overstressed legs and arms. The Commissioner and his crew crowd around Poco to harvest comments about the uniform experiment. With Paul Alexander standing by, Poco measures his words, "We sure drew a crowd and we'll have to wait and see if the novelty wears off."

Poco leads the delegation outside to allow players more room to shower and dress. I suspect he doesn't want the officials and big mules to hear the growing gripe session among team members. Those with scratches and bruises are more negative than those who warmed the bench, mostly pitchers. Snuffy tries to put a positive spin on the experiment, "Look, boys, this first time out produced a little pain, but you'll have to admit, the new pants were a lot cooler, weren't they."

Dad leaves with the last player and I gather towels that are dirtier and bloodier than usual. Poco comes back inside alone and sits on the bench near his locker. He tells me to separate the good balls from the bruised ones, a job he always leaves for himself. He undresses and heads for the shower.

The dressing room door squeaks, but I figure it's Coley returning to talk business with Poco. "Do you need some help?" I recognize the voice I hadn't heard in weeks. Flip stands at the cage door in his Sunday best, wearing a brown derby and grinning like a mule eating briers.

"Son-uv-a-gun!" Poco shouts and rushes dripping wet from the shower. He wraps the towel around his waist and dashes over to close and lock the door. "What in Pete's name are you doing here? All kinds of folks are looking for you."

"Is that any way to greet an old teammate?"

Poco shakes Flip's hand and glances at me. An air of secrecy enfolds the three of us and I feel that I should leave. "Your satchel's right here all shut tight like you left it." Flip nods and tousles my hair knocking my cap to the floor. Now I know it's time to leave this private meeting.

"I surely missed my team, but I missed you guys the most." Flip picks up my cap and shoves it backwards on my head.

"I reckon I'd better go home."

"Not before you tell me how much trouble you've had running the team without me." Flips style of talking is different. He doesn't sound like a coach but more dignified and polished like Mr. Craig and Mr. Alexander. He's turned into a different man since that day at Sylacauga.

"I just did my job, chasing foul balls and toting bats." I cut my eyes toward Poco looking for a cue to stay or leave them to talk in private.

Flip insists, "Come over here and tell me how the team stands in the league," he pats the bench next to where he sits. All I can think about is the black bag, but Flip floods me with questions about who's hitting, who's pitching and, "What ever happened to that big ugly country boy who threw underhanded?"

"You mean Scoopy? He's got the most wins, our star pitcher," I say and Poco fills in more details about the All-Star game, field day, new uniforms and Marty Davis' defection to Richmond. The black bag hangs on my mind like a snake ready to strike.

"By the way, Buck, did keeping my bag cause you any trouble?" At last, the mystery is about to unfold.

I go to the equipment cage and bring the bag to Flip. "All I can say is Troy Jolly and my Dad kept some stranger at bay but Poco sneaked it right under the noses of those F. B. I. agents so they couldn't get to it."

"F. B. I.?" Flip looks startled.

"No big deal. Two agents came by last weekend. At first, I thought they were looking for you. I didn't know if they were after the bag or not, so I gave it to Buck for safekeeping. It turns out they were looking for your brother-in-law, but didn't say why."

"Oh yes and when I got word they were on that con-artist's trail, I caught the first train back to River Bend. Here I am ready to go to work again."

"The job's still open, Marvin. I suppose you can go by your real name now that there's no reason to hide anymore."

"No, I like Flip. There aren't many baseball coaches named Marvin."

My curiosity rises like steam in a kettle. "Why was your brother-in-law in such a snit to find you and your bag?"

Flip unties the laundry bag, rips the tape off and unbuckles his bag. Piece by piece he removes his road uniform, socks and spikes. "I think this stuff is about ripe," he holds his nose. "Buck, you can rest assured you kept some very important papers from falling into the wrong hands and for that I am extremely grateful." He lifts a handful of official documents and shakes them at me to make his point. That is all he wants me to know, so I excuse myself and head home for a late supper.

Chapter 13

The short pants have a short run as the team's home uniforms. The novelty wears off and players' patience wears thin. "I can't play baseball in pants I won't even wear on a fishing trip," complains Scoopy, who sums up the team's sentiments. Paul Alexander withdraws his company's limited contribution to the annals of baseball history.

The team celebrates Flip's return for more than one reason. In addition to being well liked, it was his complaint to Paul Alexander about having to patch up too many bare-legged bruises and scrapes that caused the short pants to disappear from their lockers. Nobody dared ask Flip why he took leave of the club but rumors buzzed around like mosquitoes. Finally, on a long trip to Newnan, Georgia, Steiner asks, "We heard the F. B. I. came around looking for you; anything to it?" Flip chuckles but doesn't answer.

Snuffy leans over Flip's shoulder and says, "You may as well explain your side of the story before the boys make up their own. Flip nods. He rises slowly from his front seat and stands in the aisle facing us. Snuffy yells, "Pipe down fellas, Flip's got something to say." The story begins:

That day at Sylacauga began the worst slump of my short baseball career. Buck told me about a stranger asking questions. I panicked. All I could think about was getting the hell out of town as fast as possible. I stuffed my gear in the black bag and gave it to Buck to hold until I came back. Not knowing which end was up in that town, I sneaked around behind that makeshift dressing room to hide 'til the game was over. I planned to return for my bag and haul ass back to my home in Phoenix to take care of some unfinished family business. Then that big thunderstorm hit. The rain rooted me out of my hiding place, so I crawled inside an empty boxcar parked on the spur track behind the warehouse.

When the rain let up, I heard hooting and hollering from the ballpark, so I figured the game got underway. I found out a few days ago that the cheering was for Digger's now-famous run of the bases in the water. I decided to stay in the boxcar in case my no-account brother-in-law came poking around looking for me. I waited too long. Somebody closed the boxcar door and sealed it. I was relieved to see a trainman through the crack in the door and not my brother-in-law. I banged on the door and hollered, but the car had begun to move, creaking and rumbling, and drowning out my cry for help. There I was, on the move to God knows where. I figured the train wouldn't move on forever, so I relaxed and hoped for the best.

Although the train made several stops, I couldn't get anyone's attention until the next morning. A switchman heard me banging and opened the door. I found myself looking down the barrel of a .38. When I hit the ground he frisked me and emptied my pocket of thirty-five cents in change, all I had on me. That's when I realized I had left my wallet in my black bag. He didn't buy my story, so he marched me into the Railway Express office. The agent in charge treated me like a hobo that caught a free ride to Memphis. I was hungry and as sore as a horse that had been rode hard and put up wet. All I craved at that point was a drink of water. A slice of bread would've been nice, but water was essential.

The agent put me through the third degree before letting me have a drink. I answered his questions honestly, but he didn't believe a word I said. The proof of my identity was resting in the black bag that Buck was holding for me. I thought about wiring my sister collect in Phoenix, but abandoned the idea. She may be a party to the plot to track me down. I just didn't know, but I'll come to that part of the story later.

Anyhow, back to Memphis. The agent was set on sending me to jail for stealing a ride without buying a ticket. I said I could clear up this mess with one telephone call. He returned my change and pointed to the pay phone on the wall. With too little change to call long distance, I took a chance and called Buck's house collect. His sister answered the telephone. She said that she wouldn't accept the charges and her mother was asleep. Buck was not there and J. D. was at work.

"Sorry 'bout that."

"It's all right, Buck, not your fault." Flip continues his story.

I gave up but kept on talking after she hung up, trying to get my wits together. The agent got busy with a customer. Here was my chance. I kept up the pretend telephone conversation and edged closer to the door, as far as the cord would reach. Then when the agent went to the platform to weigh a package, I dropped the receiver and ran like Digger stealing second base. I slipped between trains and high-tailed it across the street and ducked into an alley.

My stomach was setting on empty, resting against my backbone. Surely there would be some food somewhere in this alley behind a row of stores. I spied a colored gentleman sitting on a crate at the backdoor of a café. I must have appeared real scary because his eyes popped open like two cue balls when I approached. When I told him I was looking for something to eat, he handed me his unfinished bowl of stew. "I'm done with this," he said and took off running down the alley. I gobbled down his leftovers quicker 'n lightning. A man appeared behind the café screen door and demanded to know where I came from. "You ran off my dishwasher and took his lunch, so who's gonna pay for what you ate?"

Half a bowl of stew didn't go very far, so I offered to wash dishes for more food. While bussing tables and doing the lunch dishes, the owner offered me a work-for-food job. I told him I needed money to get to Phoenix and I would pay him back. "I've heard that before. I'm still holding I.O.U.'s from bums like you that go back ten years or more." Now, for a fellow who's always had money jingling in his pocket and friends he could count on in a tight, I had nowhere to turn. Pilfering some food and tips left on the tables crossed my mind, but I didn't need the Memphis police chasing me down. Besides, the owner of the café was a bull of a man who would clean my greens if I crossed him.

Trying to get my bearings, I talked to customers as I cleared off tables. A man told me the highway to Phoenix was just across the river. "You can see the bridge from here," he pointed out the café window. I take the dishes to the kitchen and stuff some leftover bread in my pockets. I sneak out the back door and head west over the Mississippi. After crossing the bridge afoot, I hitch a ride on a cattle truck. By the time he let me off in Texas I smelled like a polecat, looked like a tramp and felt like I'd slept in the bottom of a sheep-dip trough. It took several days to hitchhike the rest of the way.

When I got to Phoenix, I walked a couple miles to my old neighborhood. My clothes were a mess, but I got a shave, a haircut and shoeshine on credit from a barber I know.

I know you guys are thinking, "Why didn't I go to my sister's house and get cleaned up?" That brings me back to why I hide out from my brother-in-law. He's a crook after my sister's money and he can't touch a penny as long as I'm alive.

Flip pauses to allow the gasps of shock die down. Digger's eyes pop wide open. "Do you mean, he wanted to kill you?"

"That's what I figured at the time. But let me get on with the story and you'll get the picture."

Buck may find this hard to believe, but I was once a batboy. It was about ten years ago in Bend, Oregon, where my father's timber company sponsored a baseball team. Before the war broke out, our team turned pro and joined a class D league. Poco Walker came over from St. Louis to be our manager. By that time I was a little too old to be batboy, so I volunteered to help out with the equipment on game days. My dad told Poco that I could help him if I didn't get in the way. "The very minute Marvin becomes a pest, I'll put him back to work in the sawmill."

"Marvin!" the players laugh.

"All right boys, no cracks about the name. My first name is Philip, but the Bend team shortened it to Flip. Are you boys ready to hear the rest of this western saga or not?"

"Just skip to the part about your sister's husband wanting to do you in," Steiner says.

"You'll hear it all, Squat, or nothing."

"All, all," yell the players.

"All right, now where was I? Oh yes."

I was just getting the hang of coaching the team when the draft board sent greetings to Poco and most of the players on the team. Two weeks later I was called up and the Bend Rangers folded. The league fell apart. I completed basic training and headed for England when the Red Cross informed me my father had been crushed by a logging truck and might not survive. By the time I arrived home my father had died leaving my mother in shock and my younger sister swishing out of control like a knuckleball. The army discharged me to take care of my family. It was up to me to handle the business, but my mind had been on baseball instead of cutting timber. We sold out lock, stock and barrel.

My mother's grieving never let up, so we moved her back to her home town. Within a month of moving to Phoenix she collapsed and died from a stroke within weeks.

This next part gets a little complicated so bear with me. After selling the company, our lawyer created a trust to protect mother from "banjo-pickers" that might woo her for her money. When she died, my sister and I inherited everything. Both of us could survive comfortably without having to work.

I hung around big league spring training camps around Arizona hoping to follow my dream to become a coach. One day after the war, I ran into Poco who was searching for a manager's job. We teamed up and word came that a new class D league was gearing up here in the South. A few days later we rounded up a couple of unemployed players and headed to River Bend.

"So that's how you got here but why'd you desert us all of a sudden?" Stretch Slagle asks.

"And what happened to your sister?"

Flip sighs, "She followed her dream and I followed mine. This is what happened:"

Dorothy discovered Las Vegas. She tried to break into show business, but she met a gambler and got married instead. I was so busy with my own life that I didn't realize the roulette wheels had spun a web they couldn't escape from. Instead of striking it rich, the bum squandered my sister's allowance. All they had left every month was a handful of I.O.U.'s they couldn't pay. He demanded more money, but she had to have my permission. They moved in with me in Phoenix. Her husband put the squeeze on me to dissolve the trust and split the money. I refused. When he discovered Dorothy would inherit the entire estate when I bit the dust, he began stalking me. I made myself scarce around Phoenix. That day he showed up at Sylacauga looking for me, I had to become invisible again.

Flip pauses as though he finished his story, but the players shot questions faster than he could handle.

"Hold on, let me have a breather. Time out."

"I don't blame you for leaving, I'd be afraid to show my face in Phoenix with that headhunter on the loose," Red Mickler says shaking his head.

"Well, I took care of that son-uv-a-gun when I got back to Phoenix."

"You mean you shot him?" Digger exclaims. The players lean forward anticipating Flip's answer.

"It's more involved than putting a bullet through his cheating heart. But, I'm not sure you guys want to hear what happened next. It's something I'm not very proud of." Flip bows his head as if to gather the courage to finish the story. He stiffens his back and goes on:

I got all cleaned up at the barbershop, but my clothes were ready for cremation. I needed clothes from my sister's house but I was afraid of a showdown with her husband. The barber agreed to telephone my sister and assess the situation. He called and asked to speak to me, but of course, I wasn't there. The he asked to speak to her husband. He was also gone.

I thanked my barber and walked several blocks to our house. What I saw when Dorothy came to the door made me sick. Her face looked as though she had tangled with the business end of a bull whip. I reached to hug her but one arm was bruised and the other out of joint. I knew what had happened before she told me. She was too afraid to go see a doctor for fear of getting another beating. I asked a neighbor to drive us to the hospital because that coward brother-in-law had taken her car to search for me.

It took a few days to get her straightened out and for me to secure some emergency money from the bank. Meanwhile, I called the police, but they didn't want to intervene in a domestic dispute. I called the F.B.I. to report Sheldon for attempted kidnapping and stealing my sister's car. They agreed to track him down in Alabama if I would obtain a warrant for his arrest.

As soon as Dorothy was able to travel, I drove her to Reno to divorce that rotten creature that beat her to a pulp and took her car. I left her in Phoenix with a hired body guard and caught the train, with a paid ticket this time, and returned to where I belong.

What about Sheldon, that killer-gambler," Red asks, "what if he comes after you and your sister again?"

"Not a chance, he's deep-fried meat as far as the F.B.I. is concerned. They'll get their man if he's not already in custody." Flip beckons me to the front of the bus. "I never thanked you for keeping my goods safe, so here's five bucks for your trouble." He presses a folded bill into my hand and tells me to save it for college.

"Thank you, but why the big fuss over stuff in your bag?" I whisper.

"Not now, Buck, not now."

"We're pulling into the city limits," the bus drive announces.

Poco stands facing the players. "Listen up, boys. This is important. We're here to play baseball like the professionals we are and that is all. I realize there's bad blood between them and us, but if Red here can bury the hatchet then we all can. What happened the last time our teams met is over and done with. I want you to leave all grudges here on the bus."

"What if them jackasses wanna start somethin'?" Digger snorts.

"Then you'll act like ducks walking in the rain. Whatever jibes they hurl at you need to slide right off your backs. The same goes for everything the fans throw your way. They paid for their tickets, so let 'em holler."

The bus turns onto Main Street and drives under a banner that reads: MURDER THE MILLERS.

"I'll be damned," Poco mutters, "just stirring up the coals."

The bus pulls in the high school parking lot and stops near the stadium. A lone black car is parked in the shadow of the gym. The bus drive swings open the door and I scream, "Flip, don't get out!" Everyone freezes and stares at me. "The gambler's out there. He's gonna kill you." I point at the car between the buildings.

Flip leans over to get a better view. "That's my sister's car all right. Damn, where are the G-men when you need them?"

"Now everybody stay calm," Poco pumps his open palms downward. The bus driver closes the door.

Flip tells Poco, "There's no need to put the whole team in danger. I'll go out and confront him. He's no longer my brother-in-law, so he has nothing to gain by doing me in."

"But what if he doesn't know that."

"Look, he's getting out of the car."

"He's heading this way."

Red Mickler pulls the door handle forward, opens the bus door and steps out. Before anyone can react, he walks toward the man stopping him only a couple yards from the bus. In the light I notice the stranger wears a black striped suit, black shirt with a dingy white tie and black and white shoes. His cocked fedora completes the picture of gamblers I've seen in the movies.

"That's Sheldon all right," Flip says, "Let me out before Red gets hurt. This is not his fight." He starts to move but Poco and Snuffy restrain him.

"Just sit tight Flip, let Red handle this," Poco advises.

The gambler points at the bus and gestures for Red to move over. Red stands fast until the man shoves a hand inside his coat, a move that means trouble. Red steps aside. The man calls out, "Marvin, I know you're in there, now come on out before somebody gets hurt. I'll count to. . ."

Before he can finish his threat, Red reaches across his left shoulder and crushes Sheldon's hand against his chest inside the coat. With another quick move, Red shoves the man's elbow into his arm pit. A muffled gunshot crumples Sheldon into Red's arms, his right hand falling outside his coat. Red holds on to the gun still inside the coat. A Newnan player rushes out of the dressing room to Red's aid. Flip jumps from the bus and helps them lower the wounded gambler to the ground.

"Lemme have that gun, Red. I'll finish him off," demands Flip.

"Hold on there, Flip," Poco says pulling him away from the assailant. "You're not a murderer like him."

"Well you guys turn him over and let me smash in his face like he did to my sister."

"His shoulder's real busted up, Flip." Red says, "Y'all go and get dressed. I stay with him 'til the police arrive. I'll have to answer some questions anyway." Red turns to thank the Newnan player who came to his aid.

"Oh, no, not you," he exclaims.

"Omigod, man, I thought you were. . ."

"Dead?"

"Or something like that. Man, you had another close call right here."

"Are you pitching today," Red asks.

"Naw, ain't my turn."

"Good!"

"Are you catching?"

"Naw, ain't ready yet."

"Good!" The pitcher heads back to the dressing then turns and exchanges smiles with Red.

The day's game is more like a chess match than a baseball rivalry. The incident in the parking lot sets the players on a different course of courtesy and sportsmanship. The umpires love it—no arguments, no ragging and best of all, no brush-offs or bean balls. Even the bloodthirsty fans are subdued. Although we won the game, everyone seems to be satisfied that determination among all the players had not diminished.

On the bus ride back home I am worried. When the story of the confrontation and shooting reach my parents' ears, I may have enjoyed my last road trip with the Millers. I try to think of ways to soften the incident to sound like I was never in danger the whole time.

Next day, I get up early and fix my breakfast before Mother comes home from work and Dad wakes up. I'll go on to the club house to get ready for the return trip to Newnan a couple hours until the bus arrives. I'll try to sneak in one more road trip before my parents hear about yesterday's trouble and ground me for good.

I sit on the step and lean against the locked dressing room door to wait. "Buck, Buck." A coarse voice calls to me. I rub my eyes and look around. "Buck, Buck." It's the voice again. It sounds like the crazy bat. I cut my eyes from side to side, then up and down, seeing nothing unusual. Something moves in the shrubbery. I scramble to my feet to catch whoever's playing with my mind.

Marty Davis stands there with his hands cupped over his mouth stifling a laugh.

"You're back!"

"Yeah but not to play ball. I've come for my bat."

"Your bat? It's gone. Didn't you take it with you to Richmond?"

"Naw, I must've left it here, don't remember. I tried using one of theirs, but couldn't get my rhythm going. Even bought a new one, same length, same brand. Oh, I hit the ball pretty solid but right into somebody's glove. Most of the time they didn't have to take a step, just like I aimed the ball at them. Marty sits beside me and runs his fingers through his wavy black hair. "Are you sure my bat is missing."

"Yessir, and I hate it too. That was Frog McGee's old bat and. . ." I stop short of telling our former star hitter more about the funny bat's strange ways. ". . .It's kind-a special in a way."

"Yeah, kind-a special, like when I'd go to the on-deck circle and take a knee. . ."

"And, and," I say as he pauses. I know what he's trying to say, but he won't go through with it. Maybe he thinks I'm too interested or just a kid who won't understand.

"Let's just say me and that bat became hitting fools and I don't understand why. It's sort of strange, you might say it's a mystic bat."

"Yessir, a mystic bat, all right."

Chapter 14

Mother comes in from work, slams the front door and stands over my bed breathing fire. "That's the last out of town trip for you, young man! You could've been killed!" From the tone of Mother's voice, I know her threats leave no room for "yes buts" from me. The shooting at Newnan finally made the rounds of the spooler room gossip circle. Mother goes on barking orders like a drill sergeant, her words flying too fast for my sleep-shackled mind to bear. But the message is clear, I am grounded. No more road trips for this batboy.

My sisters pretend to be asleep, but they giggle, hit the floor and follow Mother like ducklings into the kitchen. Lying here alone waiting for disappointment to wash out of my head, I wait for Dad to come and lift my spirits. Instead, I hear Mother fussing at him for not telling her about my narrow escape from death at Newnan. I get out of bed and take my troubles to the front porch swing. A slight breeze brushes the warm air of July across my bare chest as I ponder my fate.

Why can't people just enjoy baseball games without worrying about making money?

Why can't Mother rekindle her lost spark for baseball and quit harping on my love for the game?

Why are pitchers such a miserable bunch of clowns?

Why can't girls play baseball?

Why can't colored people sit in the shade to watch baseball games?

Why do some players refuse to grow up and keep on treating their batboy like a slave?

These questions buzzing 'round my head are getting me down on the game. Maybe next season I'll take my place on the dugout roof and enjoy watching baseball again without worrying about Frog McGee's mystic bat. The team plays at home today, so I'll eat breakfast and try to shift my thoughts back to Briers Field.

On the way to the clubhouse, I spot Tad in his yard and ask if he would like to help me. "You mean be the batboy?" his eyes widen.

"Like you'll be assistant batboy."

After telling his mother, Tad skips beside me like a hungry puppy. When we arrive at the dressing room, I ask Flip if Tad can team up with me. He says I need to get Poco's O. K., but he is busy talking with Marty in the equipment cage. Marty confesses he failed to make the team at Richmond and he pleads with Poco to take him back.

"We'll see, Marty. Sit this game out and I'll take it up with the club owners tonight. Money's kind-a tight right now."

Poco gives a nod to Tad's new job, so I break him in by letting him tote the bat bag to the field. "You take the bats and I'll be along as soon as I put clean towels in the lockers."

Marty Davis is the last one to dress out. He searches every locker and probes around the equipment cage looking for his missing bat. "It has to be here somewhere," he says over and over. I lock the dressing room door behind us as we head for the ballpark together. Batting practice is almost over when we arrive.

I adjust the row of bats that Tad had already laid out. Flip tells Marty to grab a bat and hit a few.

"But Poco said for me to sit this one out."

"I know, but this is just batting practice," Flip gestures for Marty to get to the plate. Marty hunches his shoulders and saunters to the dugout. Tad meets him halfway and offers two bats.

"Here you go, Mr. Marty, one to hit with and one to warm-up with." Tad purses his lips and repeats what he'd heard me say many times before. He is all serious.

Marty takes only one bat and exclaims, "Be damned! Where you get this bat, boy? I've looked everywhere for it." I rush over to see if it is actually the mystic bat, but Marty is already swinging it over his head.

"Watch out, Buck, me 'n my bat's gonna put on a slugging clinic."

While Marty blasts away at every pitch, I ask Tad, "Where did you get that bat? It wasn't in the bag."

"I know, I found it in the dugout. I dumped the bats on the ground and started lining them up like you always did. Then I backed up to let the men choose theirs since I don't know who hits with what bat. When you and Marty came through the gate the weirdest thing happened. Somebody told me, 'Look behind the bench.' I saw the tip of a bat stuck behind the wall of the dugout. I pulled it out, picked up another bat and took them to Marty."

"Who told you to look behind the bench?"

"I didn't see anybody, but it sounded like somebody whispering from far away. Lots of players were around. It could've been anybody."

"Did you get a good look at that bat you found?"

"Naw, but it seemed longer than the others."

I figure it's time to show Tad he has just handled the bat his daddy used to hit with, but Marty holds on to it like a security blanket the rest of the game. Back in the dressing room while Marty's in the shower, I take Tad into the equipment cage and show him the initial carved on the end of the bat.

"This bat belonged to your daddy." Tad's eyes become moist as he traces the initial with his finger. I regret not telling him about the bat before. "It's a very special bat, Tad, with power in it I've never seen before."

He props the bat on his shoulder and assumes a hitter's stance. "Yeah, I know, because my daddy was the best hitter on the Sluggers' team."

"You'll be glad to know that your daddy's bat is sort-a magic. It made Marty Davis the best hitter on the team." Tad jerks around and glares at me like a cornered bobcat. "Cross my heart and hope to die if it's not true." After running my fingers across my chest and raising my hand, Tad shakes his head.

"That's a lie Buck. My daddy was a good hitter because he had a good eye and was strong as a mule. This bat had nothing to do with it. He could've hit with a broomstick, my mother says." Tad pushes the bat against my chest and wipes his hands on his pants and rushes out the door. I wonder if revealing the bat's secret to Tad will break its spell.

I am surprised to see Tad waiting for me outside the clubhouse door. We head home beneath a canopy of poplar trees waving their yellowing leaves in the hot summer breeze. Whiffs of pine kindling from a stove or wash pot make the air seem livelier than usual, reminds me that fall is just around the corner.

"School starts soon," Tad breaks the silence.

"Don't remind me. When summer's gone the baseball season is over."

"Do we play tomorrow?"

"Yeah, remember the lights went out at the field last time we played Lanett. It was in the fourth inning, so we have to finish that game before starting the second one."

Next day, the dressing room is like a minefield with tempers exploding like the transformers the night the lights went out. Poco and Smitty are arguing nose to nose like they do sometimes in a game. The players are hot under their collars too.

"But you said we can pick up where we left off, not start all over!" Poco yells in Smitty's face.

"I admit I was out of line, but the Commissioner overruled me. He cancelled the game like a rain-out. We start with the first inning and play a double-header today."

"Start over? But, I had a no-hitter going," says Steiner.

"And my home run won't count?" asks Marty.

"What's that?" Digger enters the fracas. "Did I hear you right? Start over? But, we were three runs ahead. Smitty, as usual you're full of crap."

"That's it boys, I'm outta here. Keep it up and I'll throw the next one that smarts off out of the game before it even starts." Smitty wedges his cap tighter on his head and slams the door behind him.

Poco doesn't bother to calm down his players this time. He is upset with the ruling. Tad and I hustle to load up and get out of the stormy dressing room with haste. Flip gathers his stuff and follows us outside. "I don't have a good feeling about this day, boys. J. D. has to work 'til two and Bull is on duty at the station, so I have to recruit somebody to keep score and announce the line-up as well."

Fuzzy Wetzel drops by the dugout during the opposing team's infield practice to offer his usual good wishes for a win. "Hey, Poco, what's going on? I haven't heard so much cussing since boot camp."

Before Poco answers, Steiner spouts off, "That tub-o-lard Smitty double-crossed us. He won't count the innings we played the night the power went out. He wiped out my no-hitter and Marty's home run."

Flip tries to correct the accusation, but other players join in the fray. Fuzzy tells Poco, "I'll straighten Smitty out. Where is the weasel?" He searches the field and grandstand for the umpire. With no luck, he wanders among the gathering fans gesturing like last week's revival preacher. The two umpires enter the field through the player's gate and the crowd boos, not the casual booing they are used to hearing, but vicious cat-calls and insults sprinkled throughout.

With no announcer in the booth, Smitty bellows the names of pitchers and catchers for both sides and concludes with, "This is inning number one. Batter up!"

"No, no," protests the crowd, spreading their five fingers. "It's the fifth inning."

"How much you gettin' paid?"

"Hey ump, I hear yo' momma barking for you to come home."

"Kill the umpires, string 'em up."

"Here's some money, go buy some specs." A handful of pennies fly through the screen onto the field.

The game gets underway, but the taunts continue throughout the first game. The umpires switch positions for the second game with Smitty's partner behind the plate. The change calms down the crowd a bit until Smitty calls a Miller runner out stealing second late in the close game. Flip warns Poco that something has to be done to calm the raging storm in the grandstand.

"Yeah, you're right, this crowds getting out of hand. Snuffy, you're up next. See if you can calm them down."

Snuffy stands in the on-deck circle and raises his hands. When he gets the crowd's attention, he pumps his palms up and down. Ignoring his call for calm, the fans increase the volume like sharks that smell blood in a feeding frenzy.

The Lanett Weavers come to bat the top of the last inning trailing 1-0. Some of the more belligerent Miller fans drift toward the exits as if to leave, but Flip is disturbed by what he sees. He suggests that Poco do something to slow the game to give those hot heads a chance to cool off. Poco calls time and confers with the umpires and the Lanett manager for a longer than normal session. Snuffy kills some time returning to the dugout to "repair" a shin guard that miraculously fixes itself. Stretch Slagle fakes a cramp that takes a while to rub away. Poco changes pitchers twice, one after each batter.

Scoopy returns to the dugout after being relieved. "Seems to me our fans turned into animals for no reason at all."

"I'd bet they don't even remember what they're mad about," Flip says.

Steiner adds, "Boy, something got in their craw today. I've never seen the likes of this madness." He acts as though his loose tongue had not fueled the fire in the stands.

On a signal from Poco, Dad and Troy Jolly leave their posts in the press box and take positions at each of the gates to the grandstand. A pop-up to shortstop ends the game. Dad and Troy close the gates but not before an handful of angry men squeeze through and surge toward Smitty. Red Mickler leads fellow team members to form a barrier between the hooligans and the umpires. Realizing their attack is futile, the bloodthirsty men rush out through the maintenance gate.

Poco and Flip escort the umpires to the player's gate to mix with the departing Lanett Weavers. I tell Tad to get the bats while I fetch Snuffy's equipment. We lag behind Poco, Flip and the umpires who are safely imbedded among the Weavers moving to their waiting bus. The fans gathered outside bristle as they watch the Lanett team board the bus. After the bus drives off, Poco and Flip, now joined by Red Mickler and Snuffy Veasy escort the umpires to their car.

"There they are!" a man shouts, "Let's get 'em." The battle cry sets off a flurry of drink bottles that crash around our feet. Snuffy snatches his face mask from my hands and grabs a bat from the bag. Tad and I duck behind a tree.

Snuffy dons his facemask and waves the bat in the air. "All right, boys, that's far enough," he yells at a dozen advancing men. "Sonny, Brewer, Billy, y'all drop those bottles and go on home." Hearing their names, three men back away, but others keep coming. Snuffy moves in front of the umpires and swings the bat over his head. One man breaks toward them and Snuffy trips him up with the bat. Red Mickler tackles another charging assailant. The attack loses steam and the others back off standing motionless in the background. The battle ends so Poco and Red escort the umpires to a car. They dump their gear in the trunk and Smitty darts to the driver's side to make his getaway. A bottle comes wobbling high in the air and hits with a muffled thump.

"Smitty, Smitty," the other umpire bellows. Poco and Red rush to the car and find Smitty on the ground.

Snuffy raises his bat and asks, "Who threw that bottle?" The remaining men drop their bottles and fade silently into the village.

I push through the team and see Poco and Red crouched over a blue form lying on the grass removing his black bow tie and loosening his collar. Blood trickles from his head and forms a pool just below his right ear. A broken Nehi bottle lays nearby, evidence of a good game turned ugly.

"Is he breathing?" Red asks.

"Yes, but barely. Call an ambulance quick." Poco says.

"There's no time," the other umpire says. "Lay him on the backseat and I'll drive to the hospital."

Flip volunteers to go along and stop the bleeding. Fuzzy Wetzel crawls into the car also, a strange move by the one who set the mindless mob off on its rage of terror.

I watch the umpire's car roll out of sight and a hand grips my shoulder, making my hair stand on end. "Let's go home, Buck. You've had enough baseball for one day."

"But I have to help Tad with the equipment."

"Let him take care of the bats. I'll tell Mickler to take care of his stuff." Seeing Smitty lying in a bloody heap turned my stomach, so I don't argue. Dad has a word with Red and we start towards home.

"Why were those guys so mad during the game, Dad?

"Can't rightly say, I came in late. What do you think?"

"Poco and the team worked up a steam in the dressing room and brought their mad to the ballpark. It seems like Mr. Wetzel spread it to the fans in the grandstand. After the game started our team got over it, but the fans didn't."

"So they took it out on the umpires."

"Yessir, but why?"

"It's not easy to explain. I suppose it's because baseball is an intense sport played in sort of a fishbowl where every move on the field is blown up bigger than life. I remember how my hits, runs and close plays pumped me up and the fans' approval sent my head even higher in the clouds. But my errors, strikeouts and stupid mistakes brought me back lower that a snake's belly. Some fans wanted to reach out and pat me on the back hoping I'd do better next time, but being human they took up with those that stayed on my back 'til I made a good play or got a hit."

"But what if a player doesn't make a good play or get a hit next time?"

“Fans have elephant memories. You’re a loser until you pull out of the slump. The longer the slump the deeper the pit you have to crawl out of.”

“What about the winners?”

“They get to hang the moon, polish the stars and settle dust with a gentle rain. But the moon comes and goes, the stars hide behind clouds and dust returns in a dry spell.”

“But we won the second game today and the crowd stayed mad.”

“Remember, baseball is not all that goes on in people’s minds. They work for a living and that comes first. You wouldn’t know this, but the only reason I went to work at Cherokee Mill was so I could play ball. When I came back from the army things had changed. I needed the job to take care of you, your mother and your sisters. That’s when baseball dropped to third place and became nothing more to me than a game. That’s why umpires say ‘play ball’ instead of ‘get to work’.”

“I still don’t get the connection between work and throwing bottles at umpires.”

“Hmm, it probably goes back to yesterday. The mill office sent word we’re going on three-day weeks for a while. Short time puts pressure on everybody to tighten their belts. I suspect some of the men brought their troubles to Briers Field and let them loose. With hair trigger nerves, it didn’t take much to set them off.”

“And they took out their madness on poor Smitty, right?”

Dad shakes his head and walks on in silence for a few minutes before answering. “You’re right, Buck. And it just occurred to me we’d better tell your mother right off about the bottle throwing when we get home. She won't be happy to hear it."

"I know, she found out about Newnan and blessed me out yesterday before breakfast."

"Yeah, I got singed a little by her fire, too."

"We'll have to tell her you weren't even close to the men throwing bottles before the girls in the spooler room spin a rumor out of touch with the truth." Dad's remark strikes a bit of fear that Poco might soon be looking for a new batboy.

"Why does Mother hate baseball so much. Is it a lady thing?"

"I don't think she hates baseball. We first met at a baseball game. I think your mother feels trapped in the mill village. We make plans to leave the village, but every time we get close, something comes up to set us back."

"Like what?"

"She thinks the baseball team is tying us to the mill even though the two are no longer related. As long as you and I are connected to the Millers, she's gonna be unhappy with baseball."

"Are you saying if I give up my batboy job, Mother will be happy again?"

"And if I let somebody else keep score."

"What should we do, Dad, quit now or wait 'til the end of the season?"

"Wouldn't that be like sacking the bats before the game is over?"

"Maybe we can hang on a while longer."

"Good call, son. Now I've some disturbing news we need to keep to ourselves for now. The big mules are talking about calling it quits when the season ends. They are tired of paying a lot of money just so a handful of River Bend folks can watch baseball. Even with the team in first place, they're losing money."

"Then we'll have a mill team again, won't we."

"I'm afraid those days are long gone, son. The winds of change are hitting the cotton mills all over and blowing away any chances of sponsoring sports teams of any kind, including baseball. And Briers Field grandstand is a lawsuit just waiting to happen. The mill gave notice last week that the team has to find new quarters for next year if there is another season."

Our little talk on the way home wears me down. I wish I had lugged the bat bag to the dressing room instead. The load would've been much lighter.

Chapter 15

Poco and Dad join the other pallbearers with grim faces on a steamy Saturday morning. They talk quietly with an umpire and three former Cherokee Chiefs as they wait for the hearse to bring Smitty's body to the cemetery. Players mill around the open grave tugging their buttoned shirt collars like green-broke colts resisting their harnesses. Several mill hands mingle with the team occasionally flapping their coats trying to stir up a comfortable breeze. Davey Long's wife rolls his wheelchair near the group and goes over to join the widows of two former Chiefs infielders. The three women in black stand apart from the men shielding their heads from the bearing-down sun with umbrellas.

It's early morning but the sun has already drawn dew from the grass leaving the air heavy with mist. Sweat rolls down my back, neck and arms. So I can take a deep breath, I loosen the tie Mother made me wear. Spying a huge oak tree nearby, I mosey over to its shade but close enough to the gravesite to still be counted as paying my respects. Peggy Sue Slater strolls through the wrought iron gates, spots me in the shade and heads my way.

"I hate this," she says fanning beads of sweat popping up across her freckled nose.

"Hate what?" I ask, knowing what she means.

"I hate funerals, I hate the smell of death flowers, I hate the hot sun, I hate that we're the only kids here and most of all I hate that Mr. Smitty got killed at a baseball game."

"Yeah, me too." I move back deeper into the shade, not because it's cooler, it's just lately my stomach bows up in knots everytime I come close to Peggy Sue. It doesn't work. She backs up and talks louder.

"Is Tad coming?" she cranes her neck searching for our friend. "I don't see his momma either."

"I reckon he don't fancy coming to another funeral after seeing his. . ." Peggy Sue bites her lip and drops her head. I feel like digging a hole and crawling in it, but change the subject instead. "I mean after he saw Smitty get killed. It was awful. Do you know that Smitty went all the way to Okinawa to fight Japs? He got shot, got a purple heart, got a silver star, got discharged and came back home just to get beaned by a Nehi bottle." I rattle on at high speed about war stories that Smitty told on road trips hoping Peggy will forget what I said about Tad. She has as much right to miss the funeral as he does.

"Did you see whoever hit Mr. Smitty with the bottle?" She asks as we watch a panel truck turn toward the grave to deliver ferns and flowers.

"Sort-a. The car was between us but I heard it hit and saw Smitty laid out on the ground. The men that threw the bottles got lost in the crowd."

"Bottles?"

"Yeah, two of 'em, one missed and hit the car."

"Oh, I heard a man just walked up and conked him right in the face."

"You ought-a believe nothing you hear and only half what you see. I saw enough to know it didn't happen like that. Nobody knows who threw the bottle." Peggy Sue's bright green eyes are glued to mine, making talking to her as comfortable as wading in the warm dye ditch. I can't stop talking as long as she looks at me. I finally stop for a breath.

She asks, "Some people think baseball's over in River Bend with people getting shot at, killed and all. What do you think, Buck?"

"Oh, I hear that spooler room gossip all the time from my mother. Those women up there won't mind if baseball leaves town and never comes back. I think they hate baseball more 'n a heat rash."

"I don't hate it, Buck and Momma don't and you know it. I love baseball maybe more 'n you do. I just can't show it 'cause I'm a girl."

"Yeah, I know."

"I don't even have anybody to play catch with anymore since daddy got killed. He taught me how to throw like a boy, but I can't get boys to play with me, except my little cousins who can't catch a ball with a bushel basket."

"I know, but I thought your mother, well she. . ."

"She what?"

"I recall that time after you won the hot pepper game when you stomped out of the grandstand and never came back."

"Oh, Momma just fussed at me for not wearing shorts under my dress. It was my own idea not to come to another game. I declared not to go to another baseball game unless I'd be playing. I'm tired of sitting like a possum on a gum stump while watching only boys play ball."

"Where will you play? I never heard of any girl teams around here and you sure can't play American Legion baseball."

"Momma's promised we can move out of this cotton mill village real soon. We've heard about a ladies' baseball league around Chicago."

"I heard about one called the Millerettes, but I forgot where."

"Shhh," Peggy Sue points to the hearse entering the cemetery followed by two cars. We stand still and quiet as the hearse backs up to the gravesite. "You gotta find out where that ladies team plays and tell me," she whispers.

The pall bearers lift the gray casket and ease it onto thick straps suspended over the freshly dug grave. I move from the shade closer to the others, mostly baseball players as they close in around the casket. Funerals spook me some, but I wanted everybody to see their batboy paying his respects.

The ladies stand respectable distance behind the men clutching their own little tents of shade. Mrs. Long motions for Peggy Sue to share her umbrella, but she shakes her head and stands her ground, just a step away from me and the men.

A short stocky man in a black suit gets out of the second car, presses a wide brimmed matching hat on his balding head and tucks a large Bible under his arm. Two young men help Smitty's weeping widow out of the other car. The spectators separate and form an aisle for the family to process to the folding chairs lined up along one side of the grave. The preacher lags behind shaking hands with older men and tipping his hat to the ladies in the background. He faces the seated family opposite the casket and places his hat and Bible beside the floral blanket. After wiping the sweat from his face with a handkerchief, he stuffs it back in one coat pocket and extracts a tattered baseball cap from the other. He pops the cap open and puts it on. The startled men smile and elbow each other as though they had found a new member of their lodge. The women exchange looks with mouths open.

Peggy Sue whispers, "Did Brother Still ever play baseball?"

"Can't say, but that looks like a Chiefs cap."

The burly preacher tugs at the bill once again, picks up his Bible and starts the service.

Friends and loved ones, we are gathered here to pay our respects to Herman Arlo Smith, Smitty as he was know in the world of baseball he loved so much. In honor of his contribution to God's gift of sport, I'm proud to wear my old Cherokee Chiefs cap, the same one I wore in the first game that Smitty called behind the plate back in '32.

"That's when I was born," Peggy Sue whispers, "No wonder I never saw Brother Still play ball."

"Shhh, I'm trying to hear."

Let us pray. O Creator of the glorious game of baseball. . .

"Did your daddy play ball with Brother Bill?" Peggy Sue persists.

"Shhh, not supposed to talk over a prayer," I whisper.

"They can't hear me, besides, he talks real loud." I take a couple steps back to put some space between us, but she backs up too. "I don't see your momma, is she coming?"

"I don't see yours either."

"She'll be here d'rectly, had to hem her dress, that's her coming in the gate."

Amen. Friends, I cannot express how much I'm going to miss my ol' baseball buddy. Most of you only knew Smitty as an umpire, but I'm here to tell you he was a mighty fine partner at work, always willing to lend a helping hand. He leaves a vacant loom in the mill, a vacant spot behind the plate and a vacant pew in our church. He loved to talk baseball no matter where he was. It was only last week that Smitty told me about the game of life being so much like a baseball game. . .

"Do you believe that?" *Peggy Sue asks.*

"What? I wasn't listening."

"That life is like a baseball game."

"Shhh, they'll hear you," I say, but she moves closer and whispers.

"Buck, you wanna play catch after this? I've got a ball."

"Naw, I don't play with cotton mollies anymore."

"Me neither, I've got a brand new baseball, never been hit with a bat."

"I left my glove locked up at the clubhouse."

"I've got another glove."

"A first base pad?"

"Nope. It's a brand new Elmer Riddle right-handed model."

"Really?"

"Yeah, I tied it up with the ball in it to shape it up. You can help break it in if you wanna."

"Wow!"

Mrs. Long turns around and presses her finger to her lips. Brother Still rattles on.

Now dear friends, while this game of life goes on and we're playing our hearts out, somebody's watching and judging our every move. He calls balls and strikes and lets you know if you're safe or not. This great umpire makes sure you play by the rules. That was Smitty's glorious role in life as an umpire, to stand behind the plate and make sure we all played by the rules.

"That's funny talk coming from a preacher, like baseball's more important than anything else," Peggy Sue whispers and glances at Mrs. Long.

"But it's not." Dad's words ring in my head. *Around here the mill's what puts food on the table, not baseball.*

"I can't believe you said that, Buck Clinton. You are the craziest baseball nut I know and you sound like you're gonna end up making cloth with the rest of 'em. I thought you'd aim for the big leagues one day. I'm not the smartest kid in school, but I know there's more to life than sweating like a hog in that cotton mill."

"Shhh, preacher's talking," I whisper but she's on a tear.

"It's like choosing up sides to play shove up," she keeps on, "Don't matter if it's a homemade cotton mollie, a taped up baseball or a fishing cork and a broomstick, it's playing the game that makes our head spin and our hearts skip a beat. But it's still just a game."

. . .This great umpire devoted his life to making this world a better place for all of us. He gave all he had to baseball. . .

Peggy Sue sniffs as tears stream down her cheeks.

. . .He gave his life.

She bends over and dries her eyes with the hem of her dress. Then she straightens her back and declares, "That's not right, not right at all." The women press their fingers to their lips, but Peggy Sue raves on in a whisper. "Mr. Smitty didn't give his life to baseball no more'n my daddy gave his life for the war. Some crazy fool took it just like some Nazi took my daddy's life." Her voice begins to rise. "I wonder who that preacher thinks walked up to my daddy and Mr. Smitty and asked if they would like to die—God?"

This time Mrs. Long walks over to stand by us to restore silence. Peggy Sue walks back to the shade of the oak, alone.

And so dear friends, we've come to this hallowed ground to say farewell to a man loved by all, one who stood the test of the big game of life and called every play fair and square. Smitty was a good shepherd just as the Psalmist wrote for all to hear. . .

Brother Still reads from the Bible. I slip back to the shade near Peggy Sue. Following the reading, someone starts to sing a song about opening the pearly gates and the ladies and a few men join in. The preacher prays after the singing stops and a woman begins to wail and moan.

"That must be Mr. Smitty's wife taking on so," Peggy Sue says, "Like Momma did at Daddy's funeral." Brother Still and Smitty's umpire partner lead her back to the car while the pallbearers help lower the coffin in the grave. The mourners shuffle toward the gate except Peggy Sue's mother. She heads to the center of the cemetery.

"Momma's going to Daddy's grave. You go on with your daddy, Buck. I'll wait here in the shade 'til she's finished her business. I'll be all right."

"No hurry, Dad's busy talking to Poco and Mr. Craig." What a curious flip of a coin! During the funeral service I had tried to avoid Peggy Sue, but now I don't want to leave her. It's like having a hot water bottle on my chest and an ice pack on my head. I don't know if I'm hot or cold, sweating and chilling at the same time.

"What are they talking about?"

"Who? Who?"

"Your foot don't fit no limb," she laughs at me hooting like an owl. "Them." She points to my dad, Poco and Mr. Craig who are now joined by Fuzzy Wetzel.

"Oh, they're probably trying to figure out how to keep the team going next season."

"You mean there'll be no Millers?"

"Possible, they ran out of money."

"Money? What do they need money for?"

"For, for, for goodness sakes, it's too complicated for a girl to understand, even if I explain it." She swells up like a thunderhead, crosses her arms and turns her back to me. Then she swirls around and wags her finger inches from my nose.

"Buck Clinton, you get this straight once and for all. You know I can out run, out throw, and out hit you any day of the week. Maybe that's why you don't ever play ball with me anymore. What's more, when it comes to complicated stuff, I can out think and out figure you too. Now you back off your high horse before I run out of toleration and forget I'm a girl. . .and. . ."

"And turn into a boy?" We stare at each other for a minute before breaking into laughter. Embarrassed by our sudden flare-up of disrespect for the dear departed, Peggy Sue cups her hand over her mouth and whispers.

"We ought-a get out of this graveyard before our parents think we've lost our minds."

"Right. Why don't we go and check out that new glove and ball? You say it has Elmer Riddle's signature on it. Who's he?"

"A major leaguer, plays for the Reds."

After a few rounds of playing pitch with Peggy Sue, I stop by the clubhouse where the team is beginning to load the bus. Most have changed from their Sunday best for the bus ride to Opelika.

"Don't worry, Buck, I loaded the bats for you," Tad announces, grinning like he had beat me in a foot race, which he never does. "I saw you 'n Peggy Sue a while ago. You can go on back and play with her some more." I feel crimson crawl all over my face and neck. I don't mind that I'm late, but Tad broadcasting stuff about Peggy Sue and me to the whole team gets my goat. I brush by him on my way to the dressing room.

Poco meets me hurrying out the door. "Glad you made it, son. The funeral held us up, so straighten up the dressing room while we're gone and don't forget to lock the door behind you."

Flip locks the equipment cage and presses Squat and Digger. "Get your butts on the bus, boys. We'll make it just in time for batting practice if we hurry." He picks up his black bag and looks surprised to see me. "You're just in time, Buck. Straighten up and put out clean towels before you lock up."

"Yessir, Poco told me before he got on the bus. I'll get Tad to help."

"He doesn't have time, he's going with us."

The double-crossing rat! That's why he grinned at me like a possum. He's after my job already. I pass Flip and scurry to the bus. Hopping inside I see Tad sitting on the bat bag in back, still grinning. Red Mickler says, "Wish us luck, Buck."

I step off the bus to let Flip and two stragglers on board. Marty slips his necktie from around his neck and tosses it out the window to me. "Stick that choker in my locker for me, ol' buddy. I forgot I had it on. By the way, I hear you've got a girl now. Don't blame you for skipping this trip."

I step back to let the bus door swing shut. The stifling exhaust wraps me in a gray fog as the bus moves out. Tad McGee grins at me from the rear window holding up my warm-up jacket. That picture burns in my mind as the acrid exhaust singes my lungs.

Chapter 16

Tad McGee makes the three road trips to Opelika and avoids me between games. Since Mother grounded me from traveling with the team, I feel as useless as a pitcher without a curve ball. There's no need for me to hang around the team until the next home game. When I start to wallow in my misery over Tad closing in on my job, I wander over to Peggy Sue's back yard and play catch with her new glove. I keep my eyes on her, not only because she's getting prettier every day, but if I don't watch out, she'll zonk me between the eyes with a fastball.

The afternoon of the Miller's last game at Opelika, I sulk around the house feeling sorry for myself. I try to enjoy the freedom before school starts, but at the same time, I miss having the team count on me. I wonder if they will miss me if I fail to show up for tomorrow's game. Dad comes in from work and stretches out on the cool linoleum floor to rest.

"What's eating you, son? If your jaw drops any lower you'll trip over your bottom lip."

"Nothing."

"Kick off your shoes and walk on my back. Doffing got to me today." He unhooks his overalls galluses and rolls over on his stomach. I easy my feet onto his sweaty shirt and shift my weight around to crack his spine. "Boy, that hurts so good," he says after every pop of his back. When finished he rolls over and stretches out. "Did you see the team off today?"

"Naw."

"What?"

"I mean no sir."

"Something's eating on you, Buck. You've been moping around the house like a mule with rheumatism. Are you sad about Smitty or did the love bug bite a plug out of you?"

"Neither one! I've got too many worries buzzing in my head, like a hornet's nest."

"Worries? You're too young to be a worrywart. What's bothering you?"

"You said the Millers might hang up their cleats after this season. Some players are talking about leaving River Bend. I lost my job as batboy and a whole lot of stuff."

"Lost your job? Did Poco say that, or Flip?"

"Not in so many words, but they took Tad McGee to Opelika. I reckon that means he's in and I'm out. It's all Mother's fault for grounding me for no reason." I ease down beside Dad to dry the sweat off my feet.

"Now hold on, let's back up a step or two. What did Poco say last time y'all talked?"

"It was at the clubhouse after Smitty's funeral. I came a little late and he told me to straighten up the dressing room while they were gone to Opelika."

Dad groans, sits up and turns his back to me for the second part of his treatment. "Is that all? What did Flip say?"

"He said to put out clean towels."

"Hmm, that doesn't sound like you've been sacked." He points to his shoulder blade. "Press hard with your knuckles. It sounds to me like you just gave up and quit."

I message his shoulders with my fists. “Yeah, but, I mean yes sir, but Tad jumped on the bus and took my place on the bat bag like he belonged there.”

“That’s enough for now. My back feels better.” He stands up and fastens his overalls. “Did Tad tell you why he was making the trip?”

“No, but I reckon the team wanted a batboy on the road and since I couldn’t go. . .”

“Think back, son, surely Tad must’ve told you why he is only a pinch hitter and you are still in the game.”

“No, he said nothing except to tease me about Peggy Sue.”

Dad laughs and reaches for his pack of cigarettes. He lights up and inhales. “Now I’m beginning to get the picture. Did you see Tad and Mrs. McGee at the cemetery?” I shake my head. “I guess you were having too much fun with Peggy Sue. Anyway, they came late and watched from outside the gate. Mrs. McGee caught Poco as he was about to drive off and asked if Tad could go on the next road trip with the team. She wanted to make sure Tad didn’t lose his interest in baseball again. Poco told Tad to check with you and if you agreed, it would be fine with him. I reckon Tad forgot to keep his end of the deal.”

“Forgot, my fanny! I’ll teach that little tadpole to forget.” I smack my fist into my palm and stomp out of the room. I figure Tad saw me and Peggy Sue under the shade tree and playing catch. He must’ve hatched the idea that I’d traded my batboy job for a girl. I retreat to my hideaway under the house to straighten out my thinking. Later, I head to the clubhouse and get busy straightening up the dressing room and putting out towels so everything will be in shipshape when the team returns tonight. I’m sure Tad hadn’t learned that part of the job yet.

The next day, I stop by Tad's house to have it out with him before going to the clubhouse. Mrs. McGee says he's already left for the clubhouse. When I get there, Tad sits on the dressing room step and jumps up.

"Hi Buck, you got a key?"

"You double crossing polecat." I clutch his overalls bib and pull his nose close to mine. "Yeah, I've got a key and I'm gonna keep it. Now, you run on back home to your momma before I take a notion to mop up the dressing room floor with your butt."

"Are you crazy, Buck, what's got into you?"

"You know what, you back-stabbing weasel, trying to steal my job." I cock my fist to make my point.

A car rounds the bend and slides to a stop behind me. Flip jumps out and pulls me away from Tad. "Break it up boys, what's this about?" Poco goes straight to the dressing room, unlocks the door and disappears inside. "Poco has enough on his mind today without having to put up with squabbling batboys," Flip's tone of voice is unusually gruff.

"Don't worry Flip. We've decided the team just needs one batboy. Tad here wants to watch the games from his free box seat with his mother. Ain't that right Tad? I force a big grin right in his face. He hunches his shoulders and gazes at his feet.

"O. K. whatever you two boys want. Come on Buck, we've got work to do." Flip leaves us and enters the dressing room.

I push Tad aside. "Out of my way little tadpole. The next time you wanna be a batboy, maybe you'd better check with me first. Now go on home before I really get mad."

Inside the dressing room, Poco kicks the ball bag out of his way, slams his spikes on the floor and spreads his home uniform on the training table. I linger near the door keeping out of his line of fire. He grumbles without making sense. Then he yells, "Flip, if that tightwad Coley shows up, don't let him in. I've had enough of his bellyaching about money.

Too late! Coley Farmer pushes the door open behind me and pokes his head inside. "Poco, you and me need to talk, outside."

Poco drops his pants and begins unbuttoning his street shirt. "Anybody can see I'm not dressed."

"Then we'll talk right here." Coley motions Flip and me to go outside. I'm glad I left. I never heard such cussing, shouting and banging against metal lockers in my batboy career. But I can't make sense of it all.

The argument goes on as some of the players show up to dress out for the game. Flip says, "You guys wait across the road 'til they finish their business meeting." When Coley leaves he is madder than I've ever seen him. The tires of his car spin dirt and gravel like a mad dog growling all the way round the bend. Everybody tip-toes into the dressing room like walking on eggs. Poco has buttoned up his game shirt crooked during his mad spell. He rips it off, buttons flying everywhere. Flip hustles to find him a spare. The players go straight to their lockers stifling their laughter.

On the way to Briers Field, Flip explains, "Poco's mad spell was real this time, not like he argues with umpires, but as real as sundown. Something's coming to a boil between him and the big mules and I'm not sure exactly what's up. Those men have every reason to be pleased with the team. We're in first place and a sure bet to be in the Shaughnessy playoffs."

"What's that?"

"The top four teams play for the league championship. You see, in the minors most teams don't have interleague postseason like the World Series. Even if Carrollton gets lucky and sweeps our team this week, we'll still make the playoffs."

We win the Carrollton series hands down but Poco seems to have left his mind somewhere outside the ballpark. He asks Flip to make out lineups and coach the games. It's like the second game of the season when he gave up after we were too many runs behind. He sits in a corner of the dugout thumbing through a Nifty note pad with a large cud of tobacco in his jaw. There is one big difference this time; he doesn't call a team meeting or extra practice after Labor Day.

School starts on the Millers' day off, a good thing because I would've been late for practice. After school, I drop by the dressing room to get things ready for the big series with Newnan. Hearing voices inside, I rap a warning on the door and go in.

"What are you doing here, son, looking for me?" Dad asks. He's changed into clean clothes.

"Are y'all having a meeting?" I ask. Poco and Flip are all dressed up too.

"No, but we're fixing to," Dad says. "You run on home and tell your mother I'm taking care of team business and will be home directly."

The three men leave in Poco's car.

Mother doesn't like the message. "Team business, my foot, It's the devil's business. I reckon he doesn't care that your sisters need paper and pencils for school." Not wanting any part of her problem, I escape to my hideaway under the house. My imagination runs wild. *Poco's gonna quit the team and Dad'll quit too. Flip's brother-in-law escaped and came back to town. The team is broke. Marty's going back to Richmond and taking Digger with him.* I work up a full craw of bad news until Dad's familiar limp hits the front steps, time for me to hear his story.

Upstairs my sisters rave over their new school supplies Dad didn't forget to buy at Franklin's Five and Dime. I leave mine on the table and press Dad for information about his meeting.

"Where'd you and Flip and Poco go?"

"Ask me no questions and I'll tell you no lies," his standard warning to drop the subject.

Two days later, I have my answer when Dad comes in from work with a copy of the *River Bend Lookout* under his arm. The headline stings my eyes worse than soapy water: MILLERS CALL IT QUITS. I can't hold back my tears like the time the team pummeled me with their gloves, the time I sacked the bats before the game ended, the time Red caught a bean-ball upside his head, and the time Smitty lay dying in the grass outside Briers Field. It takes a few minutes to clear my eyes well enough to read the rest of the story. One line stands out: *Everyone who loves baseball should show up at Briers Field Friday night for your last chance to see our mighty Millers in action.*

Dad has a mind to let me finish reading the story over and over before suggesting we go to the clubhouse. "Poco will be breaking the news to the team 'bout now. Maybe you wanna be there."

I fold the newspaper and hand it to Dad. "It's over."

"Go wash your face. Tell your mother we'll grab a hotdog at the game."

As we walk along the chert road packed hard by summer's double whammy of heavy rain and blazing sun, I ask Dad why he didn't warn me about the end of pro ball at River Bend. He just said he had a promise to keep, that's all.

We ease into the dressing room and stand by the door as Poco winds up his farewell speech to the team. "All I ask is for you boys to go out there tonight and play like the champs you are. And when you leave the field tonight. . .we'll. . ." Poco chokes up. He can't get the words out, so Snuffy chimes in, "We're gonna walk off the field win or lose with our heads high."

The players shake their heads uttering remarks of disbelief, not responding to Snuffy's failed pep talk. He hops up on a bench and yells, "Come on boys, are we still a team or what?"

Steiner pops back, "We're history, that's what. We'll be the only league leaders that fail to show up next year to defend our title." He faces the players. "That's why we're history, *you all.*"

"Hey, *you all* can just haul yo' butt back to *Illinoise* where baseball's more of a joke than a serious game," Digger says mocking Steiner's Midwestern twang.

"All right boys, that's enough," Poco regains his composure. "Let's get dressed out and go play ball." He asks Dad to carry Flip's black bag to the park. "Flip's gonna be late. He'll catch up with us later."

The grandstand is buzzing with the sad news about the team. Some hardcore regular fans surround Poco pressing him for more details about the decision to fold the team after only one season. “We’ve got a game to play fellas,” he shoos them away from the dugout. “It’s all in the paper. I don’t know any more that you.”

The men wander slowly back to the grandstand and the head umpire comes over to get tonight’s lineup from Poco. “Sorry to hear ‘bout the team, Poco. Do you reckon the league will survive?”

“Dammit, Abe, everybody’s full of questions tonight.” He gestures toward the grandstand. “Those guys over there have all the answers, but I don’t see anybody pestering them.” The umpire looks toward the big mules chatting with each other in their box seats.

Abe, the only umpire, starts the game by announcing tonight’s batteries to a packed grandstand as the folks sitting in the left field bleachers strain to hear. Peggy Sue Slater’s mother sits with Mrs. McGee in Tad’s free box seats. I can’t locate Tad in the crowd. Right after Abe bellows “play ball” someone calls my name from above my head.

“Buck, hey Buck.” I look up and see Tad’s bullfrog face peering over the dugout roof. “If you need any help, I’m up here.” I’m glad he got over his mad, but I shrug off his offer and go about the business of finishing the season as the Millers’ only batboy.

We win the game in the ninth inning by one run, a homer by Marty with two out. In his excitement, Marty tosses his bat high in the air on the way to first base and it comes down handle first with a muffled “crack.”

“Uh oh.” I pick up the bat and notice a hairline crack along the handle like it had been drawn with a pencil. I test it with a gentle tap, tap on the ground, but I can’t hear above the roar of the crowd. The fans settle down enough for me to hear the faint "splat, splat, splat," with each stroke. Marty finally breaks the mystic bat and probably its crazy spell with it.

I sack the bats and stand by while fans spill onto the field to congratulate the team. I spot Flip coming into the grandstand weaving his way against the grain of departing fans. He marches down to the center box seats and chats with three of the big mules. Carl Craig climbs down from the press box and joins the conversation.

Tad comes over and touches the ends of the bats in the bag. "Did he break it?" he asks.

"Break what?" I reply with my best annoyed look.

"The bat, my daddy's bat."

"Listen Tad, these bats belong to the Millers and I don't check their condition until I get 'em back in the clubhouse."

He is not bothered by my haughty answer. "If it's broke, I call first dibs on it," he says spitting into his hand and slapping the wet spot with two fingers. "It's a deal and the devil's gonna get 'cha if you break it."

Carrying the heavy bat bag to the clubhouse makes me wish I had been nicer to Tad and let him help carry Flip's satchel and Poco's bag of balls. He's gonna take over after tomorrow night anyway. I've about made up my mind to play American Legion baseball next summer and leave this caddy business to him.

In the dressing room, Squat Steiner takes a stab at cheering up the team with his warped version of *Casey at Bat* wearing only his jockey strap and ball cap. "There's little rejoicing in Mudville tonight. The Mighty Millers have struck out." The players pelt him with a barrage of damp towels as he takes a bow. It's payback time, so I fill the water bucket, sneak up behind Steiner and dump the water over his head, cap and all.

Steiner lunges towards me, but a wall of Millers blocks his path. "Forget it, Steiner," Ike Catchings pushes him back. "Turn about is fair play. At least he didn't soak your glove."

"Yeah, but look at my cap."

"You won't need it after tomorrow night," Ike chuckles.

Digger tries to get some players to join him upstairs for a hamburger before he goes to work at Mayfair, but celebrating tonight's win is not on their minds. The guys drift out and I shake out the uniforms for one last show to the home crowd. "See if some of those towels can be used again," Poco says, "We've sent our last batch to the laundry."

Flip bursts through the door out of breath. "Sorry 'bout missing the game, Poco, but I had too much thinking to do."

"Somehow we won without you," Poco teases.

"Buck, tell your Dad to be here early for tomorrow's game, say around five, no make it four. We're having a team meeting. And tell him to pass the word on to as many boys on the team as he can."

Poco's eyes sparkle, "So you've worked everything out, huh"

"Not everything, I've still got some loose ends to tie up." He reads my mind. "And, yes you can come too."

It sounds like Flip's making plans for a big send-off for the team with speeches and gifts before the game. I leave the manager and coach to their plans. I have some math problems to work on before bedtime.

After school the next day, Dad waits on the front porch. "Shake a leg, son, we're due at the clubhouse directly. We'll grab something to eat at the game."

"Hot dogs for supper again," Mother fusses at Dad as we leave. "Come on girls, let's fix us a decent supper before we go to the game." That's the first I hear that she plans to see the ballgame. Now she'll be able to see me in batboy glory instead of putting up with my stories.

Dad chuckles as we walk along the road. "I figure convincing your mother to come to our last game will help her to give us a little more slack next season."

"Next season? Are you teasing me?"

"No teasing, there's a glimmer of hope. My hunch is that Flip's working on a deal to keep the team together for another season, but I don't have any facts to back it up yet. Let's leave it at that for now, just a feeling in my bones."

"What about if. . ."

"No more questions 'til we get to the clubhouse. If things don't work out, we'll shake hands all around, say so long and hope for the best."

"But we still have the playoffs, don't we?"

"They're cancelled. Seems Carrollton and Newnan ran out of money too. Tonight's game is it for the season's champ."

Only half the players get the word and show up early. Poco tells them to go ahead and remove any personal items from their lockers, "Anyway, we can't start 'til Flip gets here." Jake Colbert takes down a photograph of him wearing a Bend, Oregon uniform. Snuffy Veasey removes a religious medal and sticks it in his pocket. Ike Catchings peels tape off his girl friend's picture and puts it in his wallet. Other players drift in and empty their lockers of combs, lucky charms and pictures.

Poco glances at his watch every few minutes until five o'clock arrives. "Go ahead and get your gear on fellas, we'll have our meeting when Flip shows up."

Marty yells, "Batboy!" out of the blue. He only calls me that when he's upset. "Did you break my bat?"

"No sir." He comes over and sticks the mystic bat in my face.

"See this crack? I just discovered it when I took it out of your bag."

"You did that when you hit that home run last night."

He taps the handle on the floor, *splat, splat, splat.* "Damn, damn, damn. Go get me some tape."

Poco takes the bat from Marty. "Give it up, son. I'm not letting you go to the plate with a broken bat. It's against league rules." Poco hands the damaged mystic bat to me. Marty reaches for it but his hands shake and stop in mid-air before he can touch the bat. I turn away and the bat slips out of my hand and rolls under a bench, out of sight.

Flip rushes through the doorway, interrupting Marty's pursuit of the mystic bat. "Where the devil have you been?" asks Poco.

Flip pats his chest gasping for air before he answers. "Don't anybody leave yet. We've got to talk."

"Better make it snappy, coach, batting practice in ten minutes."

Flip pulls a notepad from his satchel and searches for a pencil. "Listen up, boys. I need your John Hancocks on this paper." He hands the pad to Snuffy to pass around. "Here's the deal. If you want to play baseball with the Millers next season, sign up."

The room erupts with questions. Flip pounds on a bench for order. "We've got no time for questions right now. After tonight's game, I'll give you the scoop."

"I hafta know what I'm signing," Steiner yells.

"Not me, I wanna play ball," Digger exclaims pumping his fist in the air.

"It's not a contract. The new owners will seal the deal tonight if they can be assured there'll be enough players to make a team. So, any of you who want to play baseball in River Bend next year, sign the list."

"Fair enough," Poco says, "I'm game! Gimme a pencil. The rest of you sign up and let's go play ball."

Dad beams all over and winks at me like he knew all along about the deal. I heft the bat bag to my shoulder. It seems lighter than usual. Flip calls me back as I head for the door, "Hey, Buck. We're gonna need a batboy, too. That is, unless you're ready to sack the bats for good."

Chapter 17

I wake up early Saturday morning and wonder why. There's no school today and baseball season ended last night. Familiar aromas drifting in from the kitchen lure me to breakfast. Mother sets a hot biscuit and a strip of side-meat before me and goes to the next room to sleep off her spooler room fatigue. I pour sorghum over the biscuit, gobble it down and chase it with fried fatback. When finished, I wonder why some strange force is pulling me outside. Standing on the front steps, my thoughts go back to that Saturday morning in March that Tad McGee begged me to go with him to Briers Field. That same urge comes over me like a magnet drawing me back to the ballpark. Why? Did I forget and leave a bat, a piece of equipment, a brand new ball in the dugout? I have to go and see if anything's left for me to do or if the mustic bat's calling me again.

After running most of the way, I find the main gate unlocked and step inside. The grandstand is littered with hot dog wrappers, peanut shells and crumpled programs. Crates of empty drink bottles are stacked by the ticket booth ready for the Coca-Cola and Nehi trucks to pick up. The *Lookout* scoreboard in left center field freezes the results of last night's game—goose eggs fill every square, inning by inning except for a "1" in the bottom of the ninth, Marty's homerun that broke his bat.

Home plate and bases are still in place on the corners of the infield. Did Mr. Holly forget and leave them out there? Seeing no other equipment on the field, I go to make sure the dugout is cleaned out.

The grandstand gate squeaks as I push it open and a boy's voice calls out, "Who's that?" My hair stands on end.

I swallow hard to get my voice back. "It's me." Tad McGee steps from inside the dugout with a long bat across his shoulder. He draws his head back so he can see me from under his old Chiefs cap that droops over his ears.

"Buck?"

"Yeah."

"What are you doing here?"

"What are *you* doing here?"

"Waitin' for somebody." Tad purses his lips and lifts his chin like it's none of my business.

"Where'd you get that bat?"

"Found it."

"Here?" I point to the dugout wondering if the mystic bat had somehow made it back to its old hideout.

"Naw, found it in the dressing room. Remember I got dibs on Marty's broke bat, so I went by after the game and got it."

"I didn't see you in the dressing room last night."

"You were too busy watching everybody signing their names, so I found my bat and left."

"How 'd you find it? It was under a bench, out of sight."

"Dunno. When I came to the door somebody said, 'look under the bench.' I crawled under there and there it was."

I think of one good reason for Tad to return the bat to the clubhouse. "Look, Tad, I'm not sure you wanna keep that bat, there's stuff I gotta tell you. . ."

"Ain't no use talkin' me out of my bat, Buck." He hides it behind his back. "It's mine, no matter what you say."

"Naw, that's not. . ."

"Hey, boys. Y'all waitin' for me?" Peggy Sue Slater yells from the players' entrance. She trots across home plate toting a baseball in one hand, a glove in the other and a denim bundle tucked under her arm. "Tad, you didn't tell me Buck was coming too."

"Peggy Sue, I thought you swore never to come back to the ballpark except to play baseball," I say.

"That's what Tad and me plan to do. And you boys can call me 'Peg' from now on. That's my official name, sounds more like a baseball player—Peg Slater."

Tad scuffs the ground with his shoe and won't look up at me, probably remembering how he teased me about playing catch with Peggy Sue. He says, "You ain't gonna play ball in that dress, are you?"

She looks around. "Anybody else here?" Tad shakes his head. "Y'all wait right here." She tosses me her new baseball and disappears behind the dugout with her bundle.

"What are you 'n Peggy Sue up to, Tad?" I ask, feeling a twinge of jealousy.

Still looking everywhere 'cept at me, he mumbles, "She begged me to help try out her new ball 'n glove and I figured I'd try out my new bat. It was her idea."

"All right, boys, let's play ball." Peg yells. She runs out wearing an oversized pair of overalls over her print dress with the pants legs tied around her ankles. She hands me her new Elmer

Riddle glove. "Here, Buck, you didn't break it in good, yet." She wears her daddy's Chiefs cap pinned in back to keep it from falling down over her glimmering green eyes. Her long hair is swept under the cap showing her high cheekbones decked with freckles. I feel a lump in my throat until I glance down at the baggy britches. How can I admire her and laugh at the same time?

"Ain't this great?" Peg slides her hand inside the first base pad. "Tad, you hit some infield grounders to me 'n Buck. Buck, you take third and I'll get on first. Hey, it's like old times when your daddy played third, Tad's daddy was hind-catcher and hit clean-up and my daddy. . ." She pauses, squeezes her eyes tight and takes a deep breath. ". . .let's go boys, play ball."

I warn Tad, "Don't hit the ball hard. You should've taped up the handle first."

Tad taps the handle on home plate *plonk, plonk, plonk.* "It don't sound broke to me," he rubs his finger along the handle.

"Hit it on the ground, that plate's made of rubber," I move close for a better look.

Plonk, plonk, plonk. "It don't sound broke to me either," Peg swishes her britches toward home plate.

"Lemme see that bat," I exclaim. Tad tucks the barrel end under his arm and let's me look closer without touching it. "The crack's still there!" I can't believe it didn't sound broke when Tad tapped it on the ground. But I do believe Frog McGee's bat has weaseled its way into Tad's hands. Only time will tell if it has lost its magic spell.

Peg says, "It ain't broke?"

Tad draws back and cradles the bat in his arms. "Marty broke it, Buck said it's broke, Poco said it's broke, Flip said I could have it and now it's mine."

"O. K., let's hit the field," Peg waves me towards third base.

Tad taps a slow grounder to me and I throw it to Peg. "Nice play," she yells. Tad drops the bat, slips on Frog's big mitt and field's Peg's throw to home plate.

"Hey, Buck, what 'cha gonne do next summer, play American Legion ball or hang on to the batboy job?" Peg yells as I scoop up another ground ball and fling it into her pad.

"I'm gonna be hind-catcher on the Legion team," Tad shouts. "Anyway, I heard a rich man bought the Millers and will move the team out west." Tad's chatter gives me time to recall Dad's talk with Flip last night after the game.

Flip and his sister offered to take over the Millers from the big mules. Flip gave Dad the job as business manager and scorekeeper starting after Christmas. When Dad broke the news to Mother, she didn't believe him at first.

"Don't mess with me. That sounds like more of your silly baseball talk." Dad tells her to start looking for a house off the village, one not coated in creosote, and Mother changes her tune. She looks down at her work dress and tells Dad to let her know when she can give notice to quit work and buy a new dress.

Peggy Sue runs up and cuts those piercing eyes at me. "Buck, is it true? Did somebody buy the team?"

"I reckon you ought-a believe nothing you hear and only half what you see, Miss Firstbase Girl. Now, are we playing ball or chomping our chops?"

Tad pops a fly to Peg. She snags it, tags first and throws it to me. Then, she walks to the pitcher's mound and says to me, "Momma wants to move off the village and find a job where she can wear decent clothes to work."

"Where to?" Tad joins our conversation.

"Not sure, but maybe someplace where girls play baseball. Buck told me there's a women's team up north somewhere."

"Are you old enough to play?" I ask.

"I'm not sure, but maybe I can be their batboy, I mean, bat girl."

Sadness creeps over Tad's face like that day I fired him as my assistant. He tries to say something to Peg, but turns away to wipe away his tears. My bottom lip quivers as I think of something wise to say. We scuff our shoes in the dirt like infielders sharing signals with bases loaded.

Peg breaks the mood, "Look, I ain't gone yet. I ain't even told Momma about my plans yet." She places her gloved hand on Tad's head and turns it around. "If I didn't know better, I'd think you boys kind-a want me to hang around here for a while."

Tad and I nod.

"And if y'all act nice, I might come and watch both y'all play Legion ball," she adds, cocking her head and grinning.

"Unless Buck's got something else on his mind," Tad pokes me in the chest with his hind-catcher's mitt.

Peg looks at me, still grinning, "How 'bout it, Buck. Are you gonna be the Millers' batboy next season?"

"Betcha britches."